SAIL
FOR A
LIVING

SAIL FOR A LIVING

Sue Pelling

John Wiley & Sons Ltd

This edition first published 2011

Registered office
John Wiley & Sons Ltd, The Atrium, Southern Gate, Chichester, West Sussex, PO19 8SQ, United Kingdom

Editorial office
John Wiley & Sons Ltd, The Atrium, Southern Gate, Chichester, West Sussex, PO19 8SQ, United Kingdom

For details of our global editorial offices, for customer services and for information about how to apply for permission to reuse the copyright material in this book please see our website at www.wiley.com.

Library of Congress Cataloging-in-Publication Data

Pelling, Sue.
Sail for a living / Sue Pelling. — 1st ed.
p. cm.
Includes bibliographical references and index.
ISBN 978-0-470-97564-0 (pbk.)
1. Sailing—Vocational guidance . I. Title.
GV811.P38 2011
797.124023—dc23 2011022717

A catalogue record for this book is available from the British Library.

ISBN 978-0-470-97564-0 (paperback), ISBN 978-1-119-95253-4 (ebk)
ISBN 978-1-119-95254-1 (ebk), ISBN 978-1-119-95255-8 (ebk)

Set in Berling 10/12 by MPS Ltd, a Macmillan Company, Chennai, India
Printed in Italy by Printer Trento, Italy

Contents

Introduction

Many of us spend years and years in a job we loathe yet we are too afraid of quitting and escaping the rat race and the day-to-day predictability. Only those who've experienced it will understand how the daily commute and routine of a regular job can become oppressive in its land-locked security.

Sail for a Living will help those with an interest in sailing and the sea to escape that nine-to-five monotony and realise what options are available. There's advice from a wealth of industry experts who have learned the hard way and are happy to share their experiences. Information on career paths and qualifications are mixed with practical tips and words of warning. It is written by someone with personal experience of switching careers into the marine industry, and aims to give an honest insight in to how to make the change and to do so successfully.

While quitting a well-paid job for a more 'fun' occupation could, on the surface, be seen to be naïve and irresponsible, the long-term benefits – including health, lifestyle and peace of mind – often outweigh the reasons to stay. You need, however, to plan your new career carefully and avoid common mistakes which could jeopardise your success.

Changing careers is often sparked by a life event or feeling of discontent. It's often those who are forced into a situation such as redundancy and who have had to rethink their career structure, who have taken the plunge and been given the opportunity to exploit their free spirit. Interestingly, more often than not, they find it is one of the best moves they've ever made. It's also one of the bravest steps anyone is ever likely to take because it is the first move to recognising they need to be honest with themselves.

Because switching careers is such a huge life change, it's important to remember that the emotions that are likely to be experienced while going through a decision-making process will be immense and there'll certainly be periods of doubt in the mind, which is quite normal. When this happens, it is important to remember the reasons that sparked the move in the first place and ask yourself where you would rather be?

Because sailing careers often offer an attractive lifestyle many of them involve low pay and long hours. But as most who work in the marine industry will confirm, the key to success is all about balancing salary with job satisfaction.

We can all dream about sitting on the deck of a yacht sipping sundowners in our new-found glamorous career but in reality working in the marine industry is, like any hobby-led sport, probably one of the most demanding occupations to be involved in. Unless you are fortunate enough to land yourself a senior position, perhaps working on a superyacht and mixing with the rich and famous, the opportunities to enjoy the cocktail hour are generally fairly limited. That said, there's probably 100 per cent more chance of that happening than there would be while sitting in the office in your current day job.

A wealth of opportunity

So what options are available? Because the marine industry is so diverse there's basically something for everyone. It is one of the largest recreational industries, with statistics from the British Marine Federation showing 2.9 million adults took part in boating activities in 2010. In the US the figure is greater than 70 million.

It is important however, to research the market thoroughly to get an idea of the area in which you'd be most suited to work, and ask yourself a few questions that will help clarify your motivation and goals:

- Why do you want to quit your job and take up a career in the marine industry?
- What sort of service could you provide from your interests or current skills?
- Would you be prepared to take time out to build up qualifications?
- What sort of demand is there for the service you could provide?
- Who do you know who has a similar occupation within the industry?
- Are they successful in what they do?
- Can you see how improvements could be made in their particular job, and do you think you could do the job better?
- What sort of money would you need to earn to make the idea viable?

The marine industry values those with a wide range of skills, so the more you have to offer in the way of qualifications and experience, the more opportunities there'll be available. Whatever your skill is, there's a good chance you can use it within the marine industry.

If you are passionate about communications, there are plenty of openings in the professional arena of the world's many global yacht races, or pro regattas. If you have a particular technical skill you could perhaps bag a job aboard a hi-tech racing yacht.

An interesting yet highly demanding job for those passionate about fine cuisine is becoming an onboard chef. These jobs, many of which are based in the Mediterranean or Caribbean, can be fairly well paid but are often seasonal.

Teaching sailing can be one of the most rewarding jobs so, if you think you have what it takes to help others learn the skills of sailing, then becoming a sailing instructor is definitely one to consider. To give you an idea, there are 2,300 Royal Yachting Association recognised training establishments including shore-based centres around the globe, which means there are plenty of opportunities for instructors.

If working in the sun is something that really appeals to you, then the charter and shore-based holiday industry is an option worth considering. Because these sorts of jobs are considered demanding, there's a fairly high turnaround of staff, which means there's often plenty of availability for qualified instructors and ground staff such as nannies and centre managers.

Whatever you decide, whether it be crewing on a charter boat or skippering a superyacht, it's worth obtaining qualifications. According to the Marine Leisure Association, nearly 50 per cent of yachts working commercially around the world are Red Ensign vessels, which means they are registered as British flagged vessels and you'll need RYA/MCA qualifications to get a job aboard them. If you are looking to work onboard a non-Red Ensign vessel, the regulations vary considerably depending on the country of registry so you need to check with the relevant Maritime Authority.

And a final word of wisdom from ocean racing sailor Pete Goss: 'Take the time to really work out: a) why you are thinking of changing careers, and b) what you want out of it . . . then go for it because life is too short.'

About the author

Sue Pelling is a freelance journalist specialising in yacht racing, marine, lifestyle and travel, producing features for numerous titles including *Yachting World, Yachting Monthly, Practical Boat Owner, Classic Boat, Motorboats and Yachting and Motorboats Monthly* and *SuperYacht World*. She is also the Vice Chairman of the Yachting Journalists' Association.

Sue started her career as a horse riding instructor but switched careers and used her other passionate hobby of dinghy racing as the basis of her new career. She joined *Yachts & Yachting* magazine and worked as Dinghy Editor for over 20 years. This was followed by an eight-year stint working at *Yachting*

Sue spends 'another tough day at the office' as eighteenth 'man' aboard America's Cup yacht BMW Oracle.

World editing yachtingworld.com. Here she covered most of the world's major regattas such as the Olympic Games, Vendée Globe, Volvo Ocean Race, Mini Transat, America's Cup and had access to a wealth of individuals who sail for a living.

Sue is also a keen racing sailor with a particular passion for National 12 racing and classic yachts. Her spirited nature has also led her to the extreme side of the sport, including competing in the Mini Transat 200-mile, double handed Demi-Clé race, the Fastnet Race, and crewing an Extreme 40 around the Isle of Wight.

Acknowledgements

I would like to express my thanks to the following (and anyone I've unintentionally omitted) who kindly took the time out of their busy lives to enliven and enrich the text through contributions of their own experiences, including Dee Caffari (who was actually racing at the time). The knowledge and advice from those in all sectors of the sport has been invaluable and I hope *Sail for a Living* will help launch many a successful career.

Ben Ainslie (CBE), Steve White, Mike Golding (OBE), Pete Cumming, Ian Williams, Nigel King, Brian Thompson, Martin Payne, Dee Caffari (MBE), Nick Gill, Annie O'Sullivan, Pete Tyler, Simon Headley, Vaughan Smedley, Jim Prendergast, Mike Poole, Margaret Pelling, Pete Goss (MBE), Andy Jenvey, Adam Purser, Andrew Dowland, Annette Corder, Rob Hickman, Barry Houghton, Duncan Abel, Marc Fitzgerald, Marcus Harriott, Simon Jinks, Julio Graham, Brian Pilcher, John Percival, James Stevens, Tom Chant, Mike French, Rebecca Jackson, Melvyn Cooper, Ian Aldridge, Alan Hillman, Pete Clark, Lucy Gross, Stewart Richardson, Steve Norbury, Matt Sheahan, Dr Mark Tomson, Dr Spike Briggs, Neil Mackley, Tony Mereweather, Susie Tomson, Matt Simms, Emma Westmacott, Jonathan Richardson, Sean McMillan, Ian Simons, Helen King, Richard Howatt, Ian Nicolson, Allen Clarke, Andy Ramsey, Brian Crawley, Martin Wadhams, Rory Boyle, Karen Boss, Georgie Corlett, Mike Broughton, Dan Wilkinson, Steve Harris, Matt Dickens, Andrew Preece, Tom Cunliffe, Jo Grindley, David Glenn, Brendan Budd, Bryan Walker, Phil Coatesworth, Trevor Vincett, Gwyn Brown, Louise Nicholls, Mike Shepherd, Emma Slater, Nick Jeffery, Jan Harber, Nigel Watson, Neil Kennedy, Andrew Wood, Alan Harber, Mike Shepherd, Anna Wardley, Ivan Coryn, David Cusworth, Stephanie Valentine, Nikki Alford, Owen Charles.

Chapter 1

Working in the yacht charter industry

What it's all about

Working as professional crew on yachts used for sailing charter or flotilla holidays is relatively accessible and a great way to enjoy your passion for the water. Yacht charter is the practice of renting a vessel for travelling to coastal, inland or island destinations, and is a popular holiday choice for those wishing to explore the world and learn how to sail at the same time. Yacht charter destinations from the River Thames or Norfolk Broads to more far flung dream destinations such as the Caribbean, Far East or Australia, are hugely popular which means there are always plenty of exciting job options available.

Yacht charter is one of the most popular holiday pursuits because it gives the client the freedom to choose from a wide variety of activities ranging from bareboat charter (sole responsibility and use of boat), skippered charter (boat with a professional skipper), or flotilla (cruise in company with instruction).

Working as a skipper of a charter yacht allows you to exploit your passion for teaching. Photo – Sunsail.

You'll also find that most of the larger sailing holiday companies such as Sunsail, The Moorings and Neilson offer a mixture of shorebased watersports holidays, including windsurfing, dinghy sailing, and flotilla sailing, which means there's always huge demand for positions in the charter industry on and off the water.

Skippers, mates, sailing instructors, hostesses, engineers, sailing base managers and childcare experts are the sort of positions you are likely to find in this field (see page 14–16 for more about job opportunities). The beach teams are an integral part of the set up at most holiday centres so, even if you are not a sailing expert, but have managerial qualities for example, it could be a route worth pursuing. Shorebased beach holidays, however, are instructor-led so you'll need teaching qualifications if you decide that is the route you'd like to take (see page 64–76 for teaching qualifications and job opportunity ideas).

The choice and size of charter yachts at these sailing bases will vary according to the type of work they are engaged in, but generally the maximum size of a charter yacht – known as a Small Vessel – is 24 m (78 ft). Small Norfolk Broad/river-type charter boats are likely to start at around 7–9 m (20–27 ft). Because these sorts of boats are working on the relatively flat waters of inland rivers/waterways and therefore based in more confined areas you'll find they will have relatively low/shallow freeboard (depth of hull) compared with more ocean-going vessels that have to contend with the rigours of large waves crashing over the deck.

Flotilla yachts are those working as a fleet for some of the larger sailing holiday companies such as Sunsail, The Moorings, Nautilus and Neilson. A flotilla holiday is a popular way of cruising in company for those with little or no experience of sailing. Flotillas are often arranged to accommodate singles, couples and small groups who wish to sail together within a fleet of up to 14 yachts.

Some companies cater for special interest groups such as archaeology and culinary and, for those who like to bare all, naturist charter holidays are a popular option, as are companies such as GaySail.com specialising in gay flotilla and charter.

Because flotillas are generally run under the guidance of qualified staff from the charter company, clients have virtually all the advantages of independent sailing, travelling from destination to destination knowing they have the support of safety back-up should anything untoward occur. The size and type of yachts depend on the location and can range between 13–20 m (40–60 ft), but generally on a Mediterranean islands flotilla-style holiday, yachts average out at 42 ft and are generally recognised designs such as Jeanneau or Beneteau.

Another sector in the charter industry is corporate yacht charter, which is a popular choice for the non-marine industry using sailing as a means of rewarding staff or entertaining important clients. Company teambuilding events aboard charter yachts is equally popular with many companies finding the environment of being on the water, away from the office, the ideal place to develop strategy and ideas.

Crewing a corporate charter yacht is a tough and demanding job but provides plenty of opportunity to meet new people. Photo – Sunsail.

Charter companies, including Solent Events – corporate sailing specialists – and most of the large yacht charter companies, provide tailor-made programmes with specific activities to engage and reward staff.

Whether you choose to work for a privately owned small company, for one of the large charter businesses around the world, or even set up your own business in the charter industry, there's plenty of opportunities and numerous positions for a variety of different skills and qualifications.

The yacht charter industry is also a great way to gain experience in a fairly short period of time, and a great opportunity to decide what area of the market you would be best suited to. Many of the large flotilla companies operate fleets of yachts during the summer holiday season in places like the Mediterranean and the Caribbean as well as the UK, so there are often plenty of opportunities to pick up seasonal jobs.

Getting a job in warm climates makes every day at the 'office' much more bearable. Photo – Sunsail.

Yacht charter is also well worth considering if you are thinking of taking a gap year and already have the necessary qualifications. You don't have to be a university student to take a gap year. More and more adults are opting to take time out of their monotonous routine behind a desk and choosing adventure as an alternative. If it is possible to take a sabbatical, then this is an excellent way of seeing if you are cut out for life on the ocean waves.

Yacht chartering has always been a popular way for clients to enjoy sailing in some of the world's most desirable locations and, as people discover the delights of charter and flotilla holidays, more job opportunities are created. Because most larger operations have a big turnaround of clients throughout the season, the fleets of yachts are updated on a fairly regular basis which means the standard is generally high, giving you, as skipper, mate, engineer or hostess, the opportunity to sail some of the newest, innovative charter yachts on the market.

Although jetting off abroad to enjoy the obvious incentives such as sun, sand constant breezes, and crystal clear blue water sounds like the perfect option for your new found sailing career, it's worth remembering that working in this sort of industry can be incredibly demanding. You'll find the novelty of working in the intense heat and the long hours associated with this career will probably diminish after a while, which is why this particular option can, depending on the sort of job you choose, have a relatively short-term 'life expectancy.'

Photo – Sunsail

Top Tip from James Stevens – former RYA Training Manager and Chief Examiner

If you are working in the City and thinking of throwing it all in to go yachting, the first thing you should do is have a medical. If you fail the eyesight test for example – maybe you're colour blind – then there really is no option other than to rethink your career option. It lasts five years, costs approximately £150, and it's worth every penny.

Paradise found . . . although the charter industry is demanding, it has its benefits particularly if you opt for a job in the Caribbean. Photo – Sue Pelling.

The UK charter option may not possess as many attractive qualities as a job in the Caribbean or Mediterranean, for example, but gaining valuable experience where the industry is particularly buoyant is well worth considering. According to the British Marine Federation's latest Leisure Key Performance Indicators survey 2009/10, revenue from the Hire/Charter/Training sector reached £2.63 m – £1.60 m of that from the Charter/Sea School sector alone. This equates to 8.9 per cent of the overall marine industry revenue.

Vaughan Smedley – former Army Major and more recently Telecoms Manager for a global investment company in the City of London – said moving his career to work as a charter skipper in the UK for Sunsail was a great move. Smedley, who was made redundant at 58 years old, said he was in a fortunate position of having paid off his mortgage, and having a very supportive wife. 'It's not the sort of job where you are going to make a fortune by any means but I now have a very enjoyable working life because I have no pressure. I think I came to the conclusion that at this stage in my life the chances of getting another similar job in London were fairly slim, and because I had such a passion for sailing, skippering a charter yacht seemed the obvious choice.'

Managing to gain his qualifications to skipper commercial yachts during his previous jobs, was a real advantage too because it meant Smedley was in a good position to market himself as a qualified skipper. He now finds himself deeply involved as a corporate hospitality charter skipper covering many of the larger events such as Cowes Week and the Round the Island Race but like many charter skippers, he does confess to having to do the occasional yacht delivery or bit of teaching to subsidise the salary.

Part-time option

Because many positions in the charter industry are seasonal and therefore are run on a freelance basis, you may find it necessary to subsidise your earnings in the low season with another job. Employees of some of the big charter companies which offer holidays for a variety of sports other than just sailing find taking a job in a skiing resort for example is a good substitute.

If you are happy to travel, and want to really apply yourself, then ideally you should consider going for a job within a British-flagged company that also runs charter in places like the Caribbean. These companies often employ crew to carry out transatlantic charter crossings, and offer the option to work the season running the yachts at the holiday destination.

With this in mind, it pays to have at least one skill other than skippering a yacht in order to make it work. One of the best options, particularly if you have a flair for good communication, is to become an instructor. Charter skipper Vaughan Smedley said he would have done better to have concentrated on getting his teaching exams earlier. 'I seriously think I spent too long actually sailing rather thinking about alternatives. I now realise the more instructor certificates you have, the more employable you are. Now I have my instructor's certificate it allows me to

Companies such as OnDeck are keen to attract crew for transatlantic crossings as well as corporate charters in places like Antigua Sailing Week. Photo – Sue Pelling.

sail in the summer and teach in the winter months. Teaching theory such as navigation is also a good winter option.'

Do you have what it takes?

If you think working long hours in the intense heat is something you could cope with, what about your views on dealing with the general public and your customer care skills? Are you a good communicator, and do you have an everlasting supply of patience? If you answer yes to all the above, then you could possess some of the qualities needed to work on charter yachts at home or abroad. This sort of client-led industry is all about imparting knowledge through good communication, and being someone who can stay calm in difficult situations is also an asset in this sort of job. Because you'll invariably be working in such close quarters with clients and associates, an ability to remain tolerant is also crucial.

Annie O'Sullivan – Director of girlsforsail.com – the successful UK race training/charter company that was set up at the beginning of 2000, says one of most important attributes is being able to really like people and enjoy their company.

> 'If you are a bit of an introvert and have spent years working on your own sitting in front of your computer in an office, you will not appreciate having six people sitting right next to you for a week on your boat. Thankfully I love having people around and I really don't like being alone so it worked for me, but I would say you need to be naturally sociable, have lots of patience and tolerance, and ideally be naturally enthusiastic. Working in this sort of business is extremely hard work.'

Annie O'Sullivan (second from left) set up her own company girlsforsail.com in 2000. Photo – Girlsforsail.

You could find yourself working on a 10–20 m (35–60 ft) yacht based in the Mediterranean or Caribbean but there'll generally be a high turnover of guests which means a fast turnaround at the end of a charter period. The usual period is one or two weeks, which means you'll be in charge of making sure the charter guests utilise and enjoy the time they have aboard.

This sort of charter work is often popular with couples working together as a team, with one as skipper and the other as host/hostess. These jobs are not the easiest to find and are often more associated with liveaboard superyachts. Some crew agencies will recommend finding independent jobs for one or two seasons in order to gain experience, which will, in turn, give you a better chance of marketing yourself as a couple.

Qualifications

If you want to succeed in this area of the sport and gain your passport into a new career whether it be setting up your own business or working for another company, then there really is no option other than investing in the future by getting yourself qualified. Most British flagged companies are Royal Yachting Association (RYA) recognised, which means you'll need RYA qualifications to fit the criteria.

To obtain the required qualifications, you'll need to sign yourself up for a training course at one of the 2,200 or more RYA recognised training centres, which are based in over 23 countries worldwide. Many RYA training centres offer what are known as 'zero to hero' courses where it is possible to cover all the skills needed to take your exams in four months.

Although there are advantages to signing up for an intense 16-week training course that should take you from a complete beginner through all the skills, theory, qualifications and sailing miles necessary to reach professional standard in one go, it might be worth considering taking the longer route, particularly if you are new to sailing and have the time to spare.

Ideally, the training for this sort of exam should run parallel with the sailing you already do, using it as a platform on which to base your professional training. The practical side of these exams – known as Certificate of Competence – is based on experience, so the more hands-on practice you get through real life situations, the more confidence you'll have and the better chance you'll have of not only passing the exams with flying colours, but also being able to promote yourself more confidently to prospective employees.

When Annie O'Sullivan who was in her late 20s, quit her London-based job as Senior Manager at Kingfisher, and decided to set up her business in the marine industry she was a total sailing novice. She'd worked in the City of London since she was 18 but it was a chance meeting with Dame Ellen MacArthur at Kingfisher's AGM that led O'Sullivan to rethink her career. 'Ellen was such an inspiration and full of enthusiasm and it just made me realise what I was doing was wrong and I needed to get out of there. I didn't have any sort of plan but the very next day I took early redundancy and the rest is history.'

With no experience of sailing yachts and a need to learn pretty fast Annie got her funds sorted, did a bit of research and signed up for a series of sail training courses. For someone in O'Sullivan's position, a practical option could have been signing up for one of the fast-track style courses and passing all the necessary exams for teaching and skippering a yacht in the shortest possible time. However, it's as well to be aware that regardless of how good you may be at studying, and passing exams, there really is nothing to beat building up practical sailing experience over a longer period of time.

Speaking of her own experience, O'Sullivan believes you need at least a year to get anywhere near enough skill to even consider taking charge of a yacht.

> 'There's no way you can really learn what you need to know to be in charge of a yacht in just a few months. Sailing is far from straightforward. There are so many variables. For example, if the wind picks up to 45 kts when you have a boat full of inexperienced clients, you need to know you can cope without panicking which means you need to have experienced similar scenarios many times before to be able to feel confident about handling the situation.'

What's required

In general terms, if you are considering work in the charter industry either as a skipper, or mate, then the ultimate aim is to pass an RYA Yachtmaster exam. As well as the theory you'll also need to complete the practical side of the exam, known as the Certificate of Competence. Finally, you have to get your certificate commercially endorsed to show that you have undergone additional training and a medical fitness test, to enable you to work on commercial vessels. The commercial endorsement needs to be revalidated which means you have to complete a form from the RYA declaring you have 150 days commercial experience in the last five years. You also need to have another medical examination.

James Stevens – former RYA Training Manager and Chief Examiner – explained there are sometimes confusions. 'For example, the Coastal Skipper Yachtmaster shorebased course where you do the navigation and so on, is carried out in the classroom, so people think they are Yachtmasters but they are not, they have just done the course. They only become a Yachtmasters when they pass their Certificate of Competence.'

There are three levels of RYA Yachtmaster exams: Coastal, Offshore and Ocean.

- **RYA Yachtmaster Coastal** certificate gives you the knowledge to skipper a yacht up to 24 m LOA but no more than 20 miles from a safe haven.
  Exam Prerequisites: At least 30 days' sailing experience including two days as skipper, need to have covered at least 800 miles, 12 night hours, a restricted (VHF only) Radio Operators

Certificate or a GMDSS Short Range Certificate or higher grade of marine radio certificate. A valid first aid certificate.

- **RYA Yachtmaster Offshore** certificate allows you to skipper a yacht of up to 200 gross tonnes or gt up to 150 miles offshore.
  Exam Prerequisites: At least 50 days' sailing experience including five days as skipper all within 10 years prior to the exam, 2,500 miles including at least five passages over 60 miles acting as skipper for at least two of these passages, and including two overnight passages. At least half this mileage to have taken place in tidal waters, a restricted (VHF only) Radio Operators Certificate or a GMDSS Short Range Certificate or higher grade of marine radio certificate, a valid first aid certificate.
- **Yachtmaster Ocean** is the ultimate RYA exam because it provides the most opportunities. It allows you to skipper a yacht of up to 200 gt to any part of the world.
  Exam Prerequisites: 600-mile non-stop ocean passage as skipper or mate of watch, for a duration of at least 96 hours, a DoT Yachtmaster Coastal Certificate issued prior to 1973 or an RYA/MCA Yachtmaster Offshore Certificate of Competence, a restricted (VHF only) Radio Operators Certificate or a GMDSS Short Range Certificate or higher grade of marine radio certificate. A valid first aid certificate.

While the aim is obtain the highest qualification possible for the yacht charter industry, the most useful exam to have under your belt is the RYA Yachtmaster Offshore. This allows you to skipper a yacht up to 150 miles offshore, which means you'll be able to sail across the Channel without too much concern, and carry out some really worthwhile passages.

Although the Yachtmaster Coastal may be fairly restrictive as far as the distance you can sail offshore is concerned, it is still a worthwhile exam to take because it not only provides valuable experience in both theory and practice during training, but the process of taking the exam also offers an opportunity to prepare you for the Yachtmaster Offshore. The RYA Yachtmaster Coastal exam is also highly regarded and could lead to an entry-level job albeit fairly low paid.

Qualifying as an RYA Yachtmaster is also the first step to MCA qualifications, which are required to work on vessels over 200 gross tonnes such as superyachts or sail training ships. (see Chapter 3).

As a skipper, it's also worth remembering the importance of practical/engineering skills as well as all your RYA sailing qualifications. Although at this stage you may be familiar with the basics of how a diesel engine works for example, hands-on practice will really set you up and give you more confidence knowing you could potentially deal with problems should they arise. Although there are engineers employed specifically for dealing with engine related problems, it pays to be wise. Ideally you should sign up for the RYA Diesel Engine course where you'll learn the basics of how an engine works, how to maintain it, and how to fix a mechanical breakdown.

Finding the job of your dreams

Ideally you really do need to have a plan of what area in the charter industry you'd be best suited to before you sign up for your exams. Having a positive structure and outlook will keep your mind focused and will do wonders for your confidence.

O'Sullivan confessed to being fairly naive about what she wanted to do. The only thing she was sure about was quitting her 9–5 job in London and going into the marine industry and that was about it. Even when she passed all her exams she was still unsure what she wanted to do, so she signed up for a race across the Atlantic on a Farr 65 believing that by the time she reached Antigua she would have clocked up plenty of hands-on practical experience and then maybe she could start looking for work on yachts.

'This is when I first started to realise that being a single girl looking for this sort of work was not going be plain sailing by any means. One incident I recall was just as we set off. The guys wouldn't let me do anything apart from the shopping; they wouldn't even let me touch a single line. So, I had an awful row with the skipper on the startline. I said if you are not going to let me do anything on this boat, then turn the boat round, I want my money back and I want to get off. Thankfully after that I was allowed to actually do something but it made me start to think just how ridiculous this was.

Anyway, I got to the Caribbean hoping things would be different but I ended up having such an awful time as a single girl looking for work as a crew. I remember walking along the dock in Antigua and asking a chap on one particular yacht if he needed any crew. The next thing I heard was the guy shouting to his colleague 'Hey, mate, do we need anyone to make the sandwiches.' Then, two minutes later another guy walks up and did exactly the same. I was horrified.'

Interestingly, in some cases this sort of incident is exactly the sort of motivation needed to provide the power necessary to up your game and help you find what you're looking for. In a bizarre way the confidence and the 'I'll show them-type attitude' can be enough to help you achieve far more than you ever expected.

In O'Sullivan's case it helped her find a niche market. She discovered through experience that there was a definite gap in the market for women in sailing. This gave her the perfect platform on which to base her own business setting up Girlsforsail, the sail training charter company. 'Enough was enough, I thought. It was obvious the general perception of women's sailing involvement on a yacht was limited so I set about trying to help rectify the problem.'

She had the qualifications, a good plan and raised a bit of money through a new business loan scheme and set up her own business. 'I got someone to help me do the accounting and off I went. I started putting programmes together. My biggest mistake however, was I never bought a boat. If I was advising anybody I would recommend buying a boat.'

As O'Sullivan discovered, going it alone trying to find work on a yacht is a fairly brave move and not always the best solution particularly if you are a single girl. The more sensible option would be to gain your qualifications and keep a look out for jobs going at RYA recognised companies. One of the best ideas is to sign up on job search websites (see list at the end of this chapter) where most of the larger companies tend to advertise. Visiting and setting up meetings at charter/sailing holiday company stands at boat shows to find out what's on offer and chat about what you could offer to the company, is also highly recommended. This way you'll learn a bit about the ethos of the company and get an idea of whether what they offer is the sort of career you'd be interested in.

Here's an idea of the sort of jobs available, and the qualifications you'll need for specific jobs within the charter/flotilla industry.

Skipper – Although the responsibilities of working as a flotilla skipper for a holiday company and working as a skipper of a charter yacht are primarily the same, the duties of each can vary. The system within the flotilla scene is fairly unique because not only is the skipper in charge of all aspects of the flotilla including tuition, safety, preparation, maintenance and laying up at end of season, but also has to be in charge of carrying out daily morning briefings. It's a demanding job, which is why it's often regarded as a short-term option, but it can be the perfect opportunity to take the first step onto the marine industry ladder.

The minimum requirement of a flotilla and bareboat skipper is a commercially endorsed RYA Yachtmaster. However, it's worth remembering that qualifications needed for skippering a general charter yacht are determined by the size of the yacht you are working on, and the area in which the yacht is operating. If it is your intention to work within 20 miles from port or a 'safe haven' as it is officially known, on a yacht of up to 24 m (72 ft), an RYA Coastal Skipper certificate may suffice.

Mate – like the skipper, the duties vary depending on whether you're working in the flotilla arena or in general yacht charter.

A mate on a flotilla is usually someone who runs around doing all the odd jobs and helps get clients out of trouble under the direction of the skipper who is qualified. It is the sort of job where you'll learn all you need to know about running a flotilla with jobs as varied as unblocking the heads (WC) to masterminding social events. Therefore, it is one of the best entry-level options available for anyone wishing to become a skipper on a flotilla yacht in the future.

Ideally you need a commercially endorsed RYA Yachtmaster qualification but it is possible to get a job as a mate on a flotilla without any qualifications whatsoever. However, because you'll inevitably be carrying out some form of tuition, your employers will probably insist on some form of instructor training before they let you loose.

Earlier in his career, before he became RYA Training Manager and Chief Examiner, James Stevens, worked as a mate for a flotilla. He said although it is not necessary to have qualifications for this sort of job, having a Yachtmaster Offshore certificate was exceptionally useful. 'I was actually able to skipper the yacht when other people got into trouble. Flotilla companies are often begging for a professional skipper, so if you are a Yachtmaster Offshore, you'll find yourself in a much stronger position to get a good job.'

A commercial charter yacht going more than 60 miles offshore is required to have a second qualified person other than the skipper on board. The qualifications required for this position as mate are either RYA Yachtmaster Coastal, or RYA Yachtmaster Offshore. Basically, the qualified Number 2 should be capable of taking control of the yacht getting the boat back to base if required.

Second Mate – In some cases it is possible to step in to the professional yacht charter business as second mate with no qualifications and little experience as trainee, but it does depend on which company you work for. Some companies such as Ondeck – the global sailing/training/charter events company – are keen to encourage staff to train while they are working. Simon Headley – Ondeck's Business Development Manager said: 'Our training programme allows those interested in developing their career to train on the job. They'll come in as a Second Mate on a low salary but they may even get to do a transatlantic passage which means they'll not only gain a lot of experience, but they'll clock up plenty of sea miles which will help them towards their exams. We've had a number of employees who've trained hard and even worked their way up to Ocean Yachtmaster commercially endorsed.'

Engineer –the role of a yacht engineer in a flotilla fleet includes solving immediate mechanical problems. No specific qualifications are needed but basic engineering experience and knowledge of marine and automotive engineering is essential. Completing an RYA Diesel Engine Maintenance course is also highly recommended.

Once you start getting into large vessels (over 24 m [70 ft]) however, you have to be a qualified engineer (see Chapter 3). There are courses you can take, and as with the Yachtmaster, the more qualifications you have the better.

Hostess – Looking after clients' welfare including organising social events, and dealing with any travel or domestic problems during the holiday is the sort of work a flotilla hostess is likely to encounter.

There are no specific qualifications required for this job, but knowledge of sailing is advisable. However, to ensure you understand, and therefore get more enjoyment from your job, it might be worth signing up for an RYA Competent Crew course beforehand to familiarise yourself with the workings of a yacht.

Chef – Only really applies to yachts used for longer distance charter or larger yachts (see Chapter 3) where Standards of Training, Certification & Watchkeeping (STCW) qualifications are required.

Something different

Yacht charter is not just confined to the more popular flotilla/holiday aspect of the business. There is a massive industry out there catering for all tastes including classic yachts such as Pilot Cutters and Thames Barges.

This specialised sort of sailing is becoming more and more popular with companies like Top Sail Charters – which specialises in charter aboard Thames Barges, the original East Coast based sailing cargo vessels – reporting over 11,000 clients signing up for sailings on an annual basis.

To work on a vessel such as a Thames Barge, experience in the field is essential. Although positions such as skippers and mates are fairly limited, there are openings available.

The best way of getting involved with working commercially on Thames Barges is to get signed up as a mate. Ideally you'll need to have some form of qualification such as an RYA Day Skipper certificate, some experience of traditional boats, and an ability to enjoy working with the general public. Once you have gained experience as a mate and demonstrated you have the skill to work under the pressure of running a commercial, passenger carrying vessel, you may be ready to sign up to become a skipper.

The qualifications you need to become a skipper of a Thames Barge vary depending on the size/passenger carrying capacity of the vessel.

Working on a classic charter yacht such as the beautifully restored ***Halcyon*** is immensely rewarding. Photo – Halcyon Yacht Charter.

For one of the smaller vessels, which takes 12 passengers and under, you'll need to pass your Barge Masters Certificate, administered by the Sailing Barge Association. For anything larger, you'll need to pass your MCA Class 5&6 and obtain your Boat Master licence.

West Country based Classic Sailing run by husband and wife team – Adam and Debbie Purser – is a company specialising in global adventure charter on traditionally rigged boats, and running RYA courses. This business, which was set up in 1996, is the result of a total career change and according to Adam Purser, it was one of the best things he could have done.

> 'I've always had a passion for classic boats so when I had an opportunity to quit the previous small business I ran, and go into the marine industry by setting up my own classic charter company with the proceeds, I felt I was living my dream. Although it's a lifestyle business it doesn't mean it's any less of a business. In fact it's one of the most challenging jobs Debbie and I have ever had.
>
> It is fair to say however, we have looked back frequently and wondered if we did the right thing because every year is a roller coaster. It's fascinating and frustrating at the same time but it only takes one sail on a beautiful classic boat to remind ourselves exactly why we chose this particular lifestyle. It is truly amazing and we feel incredibly fortunate to be able to make a living enjoying what we do.'

Despite their huge portfolio of charter yachts available, Classic Sailing only owns their original Pilot Cutter – *Eve of St Mawes*. The Pursers found that rather than investing in their own fleet of yachts they opened the doors to other, smaller, classic-yacht charter companies and have now become a global marketing agency specialising in all sorts of classic yachts and ships which cover all areas from the Antarctic to the Arctic.

As well as being highly pro-active at encouraging people train up to RYA Yachtmaster standards, one of the company's specialities is helping others set up their own small charter businesses. It's an interesting angle, and is certainly one to consider should you have a passion for working with classic yachts.

At least three of the boats on Classic Sailing's books are one-man bands. The company has helped them establish their businesses, and even helped with issues such as the coding of the yacht. Because marketing is also one of the most important areas to consider when setting up on your own, using an established business to work for you, can really make a difference.

The qualifications for working as a skipper or mate on one of these classics is no different from working on any other form of charter yacht, but knowledge and experience of traditionally rigged vessels would certainly help. Also, because the chances are you'll be working alone as a skipper in charge of at least six clients, the ability to be able to maintain the vessel, to be a good communicator, and be able to cook, are essential qualities.

Salary

Because the charter industry is seasonal, a lot of work in the business is on a freelance basis which means salary is dependent on the amount of hours you put in. In some cases you could be working an 18-day stint with no day off. On transatlantic crossings for example, you may find you'll be paid fixed rate.

It is possible to take on a full time job but this means you may find you end up back in the office again when the sailing season comes to a close.

Here's an idea of what you could expect to be paid in the small boat charter industry. Please note these figures are a guide only because salaries depend on company, location (UK or abroad), type of charter, experience and other factors such as inclusive food and accommodation.

- Charter skipper of an average 12 m (36–40 ft) yacht, between £90–£120 per day.
- Skipper of a more specialist yacht such as a Farr 65, between £120–£140 per day.
- Skipper of a classic yacht such as a Pilot Cutter, on an 8-month, seasonal pro rata basis, between £16,000–£18,000 per annum.
- Skipper of a Thames Barge, on a seasonal pro rata basis, approximately £20,000 per annum.
- Mate of an average 12 m (36–40 ft) charter yacht, between £80–£100 per day.
- Mate of a Thames Barge, approximately £75 per day.
- Hostess on specialist yacht such as Farr 65, approximately £65 per day.
- Hostess on flotilla charter yacht, £100–£250 per week.
- Engineer for charter company, £100 per day.
- Engineer on flotilla yacht, £80–£150 per week.

On shore

While skippering, hosting and teaching are some of the more popular ways to get onto the yacht charter ladder, it's worth remembering there are plenty more opportunities available, which don't actually involve physically sailing. Most of the big sailing holiday charter companies employ teams to ensure the smooth running of resorts. While many who apply for these shorebased jobs benefit from having a sound knowledge of the charter industry, often managerial or special skills in other areas are what the companies are looking for.

The variety of skills required include beach managers, activities assistants, life guards, sports coaches, event coordinators, boat yard managers, sail repair managers, flotilla mechanics, base mechanics, yacht maintenance coordinators, fitness instructors, receptionists, beauty therapists, and even language teachers for training local staff.

While it could be tempting to apply some of your current skills and get a job in the charter industry this way, be aware that most on-shore jobs are exactly what they are advertised as – on shore. This means that although you might be working in your preferred industry, the chances of actually getting out on the water will be fairly slim. While some may be happy with that arrangement, others will find it extremely frustrating particularly as there will be little time to train for qualifications. Most large companies are keen to support staff and help them progress their careers but in a busy charter season in a popular Greek charter resort where it's not unusual to see 7,500 clients on average 'passing through the doors', the chances of getting time off to train for RYA qualifications will be remote.

Where to look for jobs in the charter industry

Before you set out in search of a job it's worth taking a look at some of the many websites available (a few are suggested below) for those seeking jobs in the marine industry. Here you'll get an idea of the sort of positions offered, and the qualifications needed, and on some sites you will even have the chance to register your interest and receive vacancy alerts via e-mail. Always be cautious of posting personal identity information on any website that can be viewed by the public.

www.crewseekers.net
www.crewmatch.com
www.globalcrewnetwork.com
www.yachtingcrews.com
www.neilson.co.uk
www.Sunsail.co.uk
www.ondeck.co.uk
www.moorings.co.uk

Chapter 2

Setting up your own charter business

Going it alone and setting up your own charter business is a brave move because the first thing you have to face up to is the fact it's entirely down to you, which means you'll have sole responsible for its success or failure. This may sound daunting but once you get your head around the prospects, you'll begin to realise how much sense it makes to go it alone. Imagine the freedom you'll have from the constraints and pressures of company life, and knowing you'll be able to benefit from your own ideas? The feeling of total independence and the thrill at the prospect of becoming your own boss are also liberating. This will give you plenty of natural energy and enthusiasm to drive the planning process which will be needed to help increase your chances of independent success.

If you are convinced you have what it takes to set up on your own, and make a living from yacht charter, it's worth considering the option particularly if you are in the enviable position of having some funds set aside. Also, in times when the economic climate is not as healthy as it could be, investing wisely in assets such as a yacht for a new business rather than keeping funds in the bank gaining little interest, is well worth bearing in mind. There are also tax benefits to be gained from owning a yacht used for business, which makes it an even more attractive idea.

So how would you go about it?

Setting up your own charter business sounds easy enough on the surface – just buy a boat, get it insured and off you go – but the further you delve and the more homework you do, the more you'll find it is one of the most complex areas of the industry to be involved in.

There are two key things to remember:

1. If there are paying customers on board, the boat has to have a licence because it is illegal to take out paying customers on a British flagged boat without one (i.e. must be MCA coded – see page 23).
2. The skipper must also have a licence (i.e. must have professional RYA qualifications – see page 24).

You also need to work out what your business model is going to be. You need to create a business plan, which includes deciding the sort of boat you are going to buy. This will be determined by the kind of charter you choose, and the location in which the business will be run. Research in both aspects is paramount and including these important points in a business plan will help you focus on setting up the business and hopefully help you avoid making unnecessary mistakes.

Area of operation

Once you have an operation location in mind, target the area and find out as much as you possibly can. Get in touch with the RYA and speak to the regional development officers (RDO) in the area you are looking at. Find out if there are other similar businesses in the vicinity; what the competition is like, or if there are any plans for other charter businesses being put forward. If there is no competition, find out why. Are there reasons you need to be aware of, or is it a niche location that's not been discovered yet? The more research you do in the initial stages the clearer the picture you'll have.

If you do discover negative aspects, be prepared to change your mind and don't settle for something you are unsure about. Remember, you will be investing a great deal of time and money into this project so you want it to be as near perfect as possible. Ideally have Plan B ready to put into operation and repeat the research process if necessary.

Type of yacht

Once you have an idea of location of operation, and the type of charter you'll be offering, you need to think seriously about the design of yacht. Unless you are going to specialise in classic yacht charter, or you want to set up an adventure type charter company covering long-distance cruising to remote parts of the world such as the Arctic or Antarctic where you need specialist types of yachts for example, it is advisable to opt for well-known, popular designs.

If your idea is to run corporate charters or long-distance passage charter then you obviously wouldn't choose a day boat, you'd go for a robust, seaworthy design with lots of berths. If it's your intention to run weekend or day charters up and down rivers and estuaries, it would be unwise to buy a 12-berth superyacht. So find a boat that fits the purpose you're trying to market. Have a look at what other successful companies use, and find out which particular designs hold their re-sale value the most. Working out how to sell your boat before you've bought it may not be a priority but it pays to be prudent. The last thing you need is to be stuck with a 'white elephant' that no one wants to buy when the time comes to upgrade your yacht/fleet.

To buy or sub charter?

If funds are available, then purchasing a yacht rather than sub chartering it from a bareboat charter company is definitely the best option. Annie O'Sullivan, Director of Girlsforsail, said

Annie O'Sullivan – Director of Girlsforsail says having your own yacht is one of the most important aspects of setting up a charter company. Photo – Girlsforsail.

not purchasing a yacht when she first set up her company was probably the biggest mistake she made.

> 'Having your own boat is an absolute necessity if you want to survive. Thankfully I now have my own boat and I still charter an extra boat occasionally on demand, but it really is not cost effective at all in the long run, so I wouldn't recommend it if you are running a business.'

MCA coding – Rules and regulations

Assuming you decide to set up a small charter business and invest in a 12 m (40 ft) yacht for example, you'll need to comply to the stringent rules and regulations which means you'll have to get the boat MCA coded. Small vessels – up to 24 m (70 ft) – operating commercially under the Red Ensign or in British waters must comply with the Merchant Shipping Regulations or an MCA (Maritime and Coastguard Agency) Code of Practice to operate legally under the British flag administration, and IMO (International Maritime Organisation) Member States who exercise Port State Control (PSC).

The UK is known to be one of the strictest countries in the world when it comes to safety, which means the requirements and the cost implications of getting a yacht MCA coded for commercial use can be high. With this in mind, it's worth finding out as much as you can about a yacht before you go ahead with a purchase. Check to see if it's already MCA coded because if that's the case you'll save yourself a lot of time and money. Most people selling a boat either privately, through a broker, or manufacturer should be able to advise whether the boat is coded already, or is capable of being MCA coded.

If you find the particular yacht you are interested in is not coded, you'll need to do some research to find out if it is capable of meeting regulations. For a quick check to see whether a vessel is currently coded to the relevant standards contact the MCA on +44 (0) 23 8032 9139 or email Codes@mcga.gov.uk.

To get an idea of what is required and to see what the finer details of the complex issues of coding a yacht entails, particularly if you are thinking about carrying out the coding yourself, take a look at the MCA website: www.mcga.gov.uk.

In an effort to rationalise and update the requirements of coding, the MCA says it has reviewed, and harmonised their codes of practice for small vessels 'Small Commercial Vessel and Pilot Boat (SCV) Code' which means you'll need to go to the MCA website, download the 148-page Marine Guidance Note MGN 280 from the 'Codes of Practice Information Pack' and start reading.

In the coding procedure, the MCA not only classify what sort of safety gear you need on board but also stipulate safety regulation, which means there are some boats that will have problems, or may not ever comply. If, for example, you have a boat with an aft cabin, there must be two ways out including an escape hatch. If it only has one means of exit, such as the cabin door, and it's not possible to alter the design of the yacht to incorporate a second exit, the situation could prove difficult.

The initial coding has to be carried out by an appointed surveyor from one of the MCA Certifying Authorities who is capable of undertaking MCA Coding and who will be able to advise on any issue that arises.

Here's a summary of what to do:

- Choose an authorised Certifying Authority listed on the MCA website, preferably as near to the location of the yacht as possible. Contact them to obtain an application form for examination/survey.

- Complete and return the form to the Certifying Authority. In some cases you may have to include an initial fee.
- Arrange with the Certifying Authority for the vessel to be examined. The surveyor will then carry out the compliance examination.
- Make sure you are in receipt of a valid certificate for the vessel before it enters service.

Before you sign up a surveyor it's worth checking the following requirements as recommended by Andrew Dowland who is one of the appointed surveyors from the RYA (an MCA Certifying Authority). This will help save time and make the surveyor's life more straightforward, and by saving time, may even result in a cost saving too.

MCA Coding Requirements for a sailing vessel

- Forward hatch able to be turned 180 degrees
- All hatches, portlights, windows to be locked with 'Do not open at sea' stickers in 10 mm red letters
- 5A 34B fire extinguisher at the exit to each cabin with a small torch and smoke detector
- Fire Blanket in the galley with an emergency action card detailing the action to be taken should the gas alarm go off. Crash bar by cooker. Cook's strap
- Piping which presents a risk of flooding in the engine room should be efficiently insulated against fire or to be of fire resistant material e.g. ISO Standard 7840
- Automatic Extinguisher within the engine room or 1 × 13A 113B + 2 × buckets
- Life raft sufficient to accommodate all persons ISO 9650 Solas 'B'. If not Solas 'B' a grab bag will be required
- Life jackets correct size each with light, whistle, reflecting tape. One per person (adult) + 10 per cent or two extra whichever is greater and a harness each
- Flares 6 × red hand held – 4 × parachute – 2 × buoyant orange smoke
- TPAs 100 per cent (Thermal Protection Aids)
- 2 × life buoy with light, drogue, floating line and 1 × Dan buoy
- Fixed VHF and emergency VHF aerial plus hand held VHF
- CAT 'C' First Aid kit with first aid manual
- Almanac – tide tables – sailing directions – code of signals – radio procedure card – barometer – efficient sound signal – list of lights – charts for the area of charter – pilots etc deviation card – hand bearing compass – training manual – Solas cards 1 × No 1 or 2 × No 2
- Search light with Morse code capability
- Wire cutters
- Jack Stays
- Wash boards capable of being locked in position
- Storm Jib
- Kedge anchor
- 2 × anchor ball and motor-sailing cone.

Keeping up standards

To ensure yachts used for commercial use are kept up to a standard in a sound and seaworthy condition once they have been granted a Code of Practice certificate, an inspection procedure has to be carried out. Yachts have to go through a re-coding process every five years, which means they have to have an out-of-water inspection.

This is in addition to the mid-term inspection – both of which have to be carried out by a Certifying Authority. Other than that, it is down to you, as owner, to carry out a programme of self-certified annual inspections, so it's worth learning as much as you can about the procedure from the surveyor.

The MCA will occasionally carry out random checks on commercial yachts but this is usually only if they suspect something is not quite right.

A yacht like the classic ***Halcyon,*** which is used for commercial use, has to be in sound, seaworthy condition. Photo – Halcyon Yacht Charter.

To aid identification of coded yachts, the MCA is also hoping that in time, all small coded vessels will carry code stickers or discs – similar to road tax discs for road vehicles – with the currency of the discs indicated by the colour, and changed each year.

Although the Certifying Authority will send out reminders before the major inspection/re-coding process is due to take place, it's worth remembering that it is your responsibility as an owner to ensure the yacht's coding is up to date, the appropriateness of certification for actual use is being adhered to, and that the yacht is being operated within the Area Operation Category for which it is certified. Failure to do this could not only result in prosecution but also put the safety of clients at risk.

Coding costs versus enhancing value of a yacht

There is no doubt that getting a yacht MCA coded is one of the best ways of strengthening its appeal in the yacht charter and brokerage market. As well as ensuring the safety of yacht, crew and its clients, a Code compliant yacht is usually more highly regarded and therefore able to maintain its resale value. Although the process of coding a yacht can be costly, the value it adds will hopefully pay dividends in the future.

It's also worth remembering that if you plan to charter out your boat using an appointed agent, they, together with the insurance broker, will need to see an up-to-date MCA code certificate to protect themselves from liability should an accident occur.

The cost of coding a yacht varies depending on which certifying authority you choose and how far the appointed surveyor has to travel for the job. According to Andrew Dowland – an appointed surveyor for the RYA Certifying Authority – MCA Coding for a 12 m (40 ft) yacht is around £1,200–£1,500 plus VAT. This would include the stability test, certification and all fees but wouldn't include extra equipment required such as lifejackets, harnesses and life rafts.

Back to business

Once you've decided on the business model, and written a plan, you then need to set up your business and have a company name under which to work and market yourself. It is also important to ensure the business you are going to run looks professional which means you need to create accounts, letterheads, and business cards. You may even find it useful at this stage to sign up an accountant to help with any accounts-related issues and set you up for your first set of tax returns leaving you time to concentrate on running the business.

In the UK, familiarising yourself with the HMRC (Her Majesty's Revenue & Customs) website (www.hmrc.gov.uk) about how to 'Start up in Business' is highly recommended. There is always lots of useful information and tips for those completely new to setting up on their own and, if you do decide to run the accounts yourself, there's plenty of advice about that too.

Hopefully your company will be large enough to be VAT registered which means you'll have a VAT number. It's also worth remembering that most yachting associated goods attract VAT, so you can take those off and make some gain that way too. A good accountant will also be able to advise on VAT issues ensuring you gain maximum benefit.

While it is important to ensure you benefit from all the tax advantages from running a charter business, don't be tempted into doing what became a fairly popular exercise a few years ago when sham charter companies were being set up by people with their own personal yachts and chartering them out to friends at a low cost for a week or two a year in order to beat the system by offsetting all the costs of their personal yachts against tax. Not surprisingly, the Tax Office has really clamped down on this and the rules are now extremely tight in an effort to stamp out individuals using the scheme as a promotional tool for another business.

Marketing your charter business

Once you've set up and registered your business, your priority is marketing your product correctly. Because you need to ensure you are targeting the right market, this is probably one of the most complex aspects of setting up your own business.

A website for your new business is not an option but an essential component so make sure you secure a website domain name as soon as you can, and if necessary appoint a specialist to build you an effective website. Make sure the site is clear, concise, with your own distinct identity and, most importantly, make sure it is simple to navigate. You need to make it easy for prospective clients to find what they are looking for. And, as obvious as it may sound, don't forget to ensure your company contact details including telephone number, are included on the Home page.

Think about your product and what you are offering. If you have a niche in which to direct your marketing, or you have something in your business that is unique that will appeal to a certain market, something that stands out, then you have a good start. Build on the unique aspect and aim to hit exactly the right market.

Annie O'Sullivan Director of Girlsforsail said finding a niche is important but marketing it correctly is essential. Although she says in hindsight she should have set aside more budget to market the business in the early days, she does feel she followed the correct route. 'Because I found, through experience, there was a market for women who wanted to learn to sail competitively with like-minded people I decided the only way to get the Girlsforsail name known was to turn up at big events and make an impact that way.'

Advertising in specialist media such as magazines and websites with promotions and special introductory offers is also one of the best ways of hitting the target market. And once you start to build up a mailing list, you can then start to market effectively through e-mail with newsletters.

Self-promotion is essential so it's important to remember to seek opportunities for marketing as and when you can. Producing a smart information pack for your customers, which includes essential company details such as terms and conditions, a description and details of the yacht they will be sailing, and key safety notes, will not only give customers a clear idea of what they should expect, but will also give your company that all-important, clear, professional image.

Chapter 3
Superyachts

There is no question that if you want to earn serious money in the marine industry, the superyacht world is a good option because it is one of the most professional areas of the small craft sector in the marine industry. Working for the owners of these yachts therefore can be extremely lucrative as well as being one of the best ways to see the world.

It is also the ultimate dream job for anyone who has a desire to experience a taste of the high life and all the glitz and glamour that goes with it. Imagine the excitement of being among the champagne and celebrities as they wine and dine aboard yachts like Roberto Cavalli's 40 m (120 ft) superyacht with its leopard skin interior. Just how cool would it be to work on Johnny Depp's classic 47 m (140 ft) *Vajoliroja* entertaining the likes of Brad and Angelina in glitzy places like St Tropez? And imagine the fun it would be to have been part of the crew aboard Roman Abramovich's 114 m (340 ft) *Luna Yacht*, with A-list stars and global power brokers aboard.

The superyacht *Altitude* has a large staff to run the charter business. Photo – Burgess/www.burgessyachts.com.

The truth is, these yachts don't run on their own, they have to be crewed by professional staff at all times which means if you track down the right yacht to work on, you too could be part of the celebrity 'set' enjoying all the perks that go with it.

According to *Superyacht UK* (SYUK), in the UK alone the superyacht sector is reported to be worth over £420 million a year, and has a total of 3,550 employees working in the industry, which means there are plenty of opportunities in this country alone. The type of jobs you are likely to find working on superyachts, and the qualifications required, will be discussed further on in this chapter but in general you'll find the variety of options huge with all sorts of positions available from captains, bosuns, financial controllers, through to laundry managers.

Thankfully the last ten years has really seen a marked improvement in professionalism in the superyacht industry, and according to John Percival – CEO Hoylake Sailing School, Wirral which specialises in superyacht crew training – the situation is improving all the time.

> 'It wasn't long ago when back-packers could roll up at a yacht and say 'gisa job?' That is not the case anymore because the industry has become more professional with a career structure in place for deck crew, officers and captains. There's also a career structure for engine hands, engine crew and chief engineers, and I'm sure it won't be long until there's a career structure for interior crew too.'

What makes a yacht a superyacht?

Superyacht is the generic term for a luxury sailing yacht (S/Y) or motor yacht (M/Y), of 24 m (70 ft) and above. And the average length is approximately 45 m (130 ft). The term made its debut into the English language at the beginning of the twentieth century when wealthy individuals first commissioned large, private yachts.

Aristotle Onassis' 99 m (300 ft) *M/Y Christina O*, the Turkish State yacht *M/Y Savarona*, and the 55 m (165 ft) *M/Y Kalizma*, once owned by Richard Burton and Elizabeth Taylor and known as the 'love boat', are examples of early motor superyachts, while the America's Cup classic J class racing yachts such as Sir Tom Sopwith's *Endeavour*, and Sir Thomas Lipton's *Shamrock V* are classic examples of sailing superyachts. Interestingly, most of these yachts are still in service today under private ownership.

As well as being known as 'toys' for the rich and famous, superyachts play an important role in the business world too with many leading international companies investing in the superyacht arena. You'll also find that superyachts are a popular choice as state yachts in many countries who use them as a unique and stylish way of entertaining. The 125 m (370 ft) Royal Yacht *Britannia* which proudly served the Queen and country for 44 years with a total of 968 official voyages, and which had a permanent staff of over 200, is a good example.

M/Y *Platinum* owned by Sheik Mohammed bin Rashid al-Maktoum, the Crown Prince of Dubai is, at 160 m (480 ft) in length, among the largest superyachts in the world and, like the former British Royal Yacht, a large crew is employed to run it.

Sailing superyachts tend to be smaller, relatively speaking, with *Maltese Falcon* one of the largest in the world topping the scale at 88 m (264 ft). On this sort of yacht it's not unusual to see a permanent crew of 18 who are in charge of maintaining the technical aspects, including the rig, and ensuring the 'hotel' aspect of the ship runs smoothly. There's an onboard gourmet chef, stewards and stewardesses, and the yacht can accommodate 12 guests plus four guest staff.

Although superyacht is the generic term for large luxury yachts, you may also hear some of these yachts being referred to as Megayachts and Gigayachts. Basically there are three main categories defined by size (see below) and anything bigger than a Gigayacht defined by gross tonnage (gt), could reasonably be classed as a ship.

- **Superyacht** over 24 m
- **Megayacht** over 50 m
- **Gigayacht** over 100 m

Under regulation, any vessel over 3,000 gt cannot be classed as a yacht because it comes under different Government legislation. Once a vessel reaches that sort of tonnage (3,000 gt that equates to around 80–85 m (240–250 ft) in length, it falls into what is referred to a SOLAS (Safety of Life at Sea) Vessel, which comes under International Maritime Organisation (IMO) legislation. The IMO is part of the United Nations and they develop international law. Therefore, a superyacht is anything above 24 m (72 ft) but not more than 3,000 gt. Above that, it becomes a SOLAS class vessel or, in other words, a ship, which means the officers and engineers on board will be Merchant Navy qualified who have experience in yachting as opposed to yacht qualified.

If you look at some of the largest yachts of their type in the world such as *Mayanqueen IV* which is a 92 m (276 ft) imposing steel vessel built by Blohm and Voss Shipyards and Services in Hamburg, Germany and has a gross tonnage of 3,879, *M/Y Platinum*, *Eclipse* (170 m [510 ft]) owned by Roman Abramovich, or *Dubai* (162 m [485 ft]), they are referred to as superyachts but strictly speaking they are ships – SOLAS Class vessels because they are all well over 3,000 gt.

Classic versus new build

Interestingly there's nothing to define the age or type of these yachts, which means variety in the superyacht arena is absolutely vast. From 100-year-old classic beauties such as Fife and J-Class yachts, to brand-new, super hi-tech, carbon-fibre flyers, the superyacht world offers an amazing choice of job opportunities, which makes it easy to understand why superyacht sailing is so appealing.

The annual regatta Les Voiles d'Antibes, is one of the most popular classic boat regattas to find professional crew at work. Photo – Sue Pelling.

Some of the best places to see classic sailing superyachts in action, and to get an idea of the sort of jobs available in this sector are the annual classic yacht regattas including the Voiles de Saint-Tropez, and Antigua Classic Yacht Regatta which are among some of the largest and most glamorous in the world. As well as cruising charter, these yachts often participate in racing, and at a regatta like this, it is not unusual to see over 50 of these beautiful wood yachts, many over 100 years old, battling it out on the racecourse.

On a typical classic wood yacht there will generally be a core regular crew including the skipper, mate, and a selection of deckhands known as deckies who will all be experienced sailors. Most of them will be qualified and have plenty of previous experience of racing. The knowledge of classic yachts and the intricacies of how they are rigged is also important for this sort of work so, if you are thinking about going down this route, the more experience and knowledge you can gain about classic boats the more chance you'll have of securing a job.

As well as those employed as core racing crew such as skipper and mate, you'll often find the host/hostess, chef, engineer participating in the racing too, so on this sort of yacht it pays to have as many transferable skills as possible.

The same applies to working on modern-day, hi-tech racing machines. They might have an age difference of 100 years or so, and have slightly different rigging systems, but overall the principles of sailing/racing remain the same.

I was fortunate enough a few years ago to be racing as a deckie on a 30m (100ft) Wally (one of the world's most beautiful modern-day superyachts) in Palma, Majorca. We'd been racing hard all day and the owner, and core crew on this yacht had been really pushing it because they needed to win the race to win the whole series. Interestingly I did notice during the closing stages of the race, shortly before the finish line, one of the crew members who'd been running around the deck and helping with sail changes all day, disappeared down below into the cabin. I didn't think much more about it until, just as we crossed the finish line – thankfully having won the race – I had the surprise of my life to see that particular crew member appearing on deck with a tray of freshly baked cakes and cappuccino coffees all round for the 20 or so crew members.

That crewmember was the hostess/chef but being able to demonstrate her skills in other areas on the sailing side made her a valuable member of the team.

Sail versus motor

Sailing superyachts by their very nature, particularly those that race on a regular basis, are more physically demanding than motor superyachts which means although the qualifications required for sailing and motor yachts are the same, the skills required are different.

Of the 6,000 or so superyachts in service globally, 15–20 per cent are sailing yachts, and the rest are motor yachts. Although this is an approximate split it does give an indication that the percentage of jobs you'll find at crew agencies will be more centred towards the motor yacht sector. So, depending on what experience you have, or what your ambition is, it is worth considering which option you would be most suited to.

The advantage of working on a motor superyacht as opposed to a sailing superyacht is the fact that you'll be working on a more level playing field. Unlike a sailing yacht which heels as a result of the power of the wind in the sails, a motor yacht is relatively stable, which means if you are totally new to the marine world, you may find this option easier to adjust to particularly to start with.

The other thing to consider is salary. If you want to go for the really big money, then opt for motor yachts. According to John Percival – CEO Hoylake Sailing School, Wirral, which specialises in

Member of a superyacht crew welcomes guests on board. Photo – Burgess/www.burgessyachts.com.

superyacht crew training – there is less money on a sailing yacht because it's a more popular option. 'My experience is that the sailing superyacht owner tends to be someone who has been a boating enthusiast and probably sailed boats when they were younger, and has now come into a lot of money and can afford a big one. Motor yachts tend to be mobile mansions afloat owned by extremely rich businessmen or women who may or may not have had any previous yachting experience.'

Either way, working on superyachts often involves a certain amount of charter. This is because the owners often only use them for their own occasional entertaining, which means the rest of the time these multi-million pound playthings are lying idle in dock. To make the owning of a yacht like this more cost effective therefore, they are often chartered out during the season, which means you, as staff members, will have paying clients on board the yacht, which effectively turns into a hotel. In fact, according to Captain John Percival who, as well as running Hoylake Sailing School, works aboard a 56m (160ft) superyacht in the Mediterranean, some of the superyachts he works on are better than hotels: 'Most are at least Six Star and some that I work on are Eight Star hotels. The standards are unbelievable.'

With such high standards it's not surprising to learn that the workload on a superyacht is exceptionally high and demanding. It is not unusual for crew members to be working shifts 24 hours when you have guests on board.

Annette Corder, 2nd Stewardess on a 52m (150ft) motor superyacht based in the Western Mediterranean, says although things are very different on board when the yacht is under charter, the theme is always the same.

'Keeping the interior of the yacht clean and tidy and super organised is something that goes hand in hand. But of course when guests are on they come first and we clean, serve food and drinks, organise shore excursions and provision and make sure they are very happy at all times. A normal day when not on charter jobs includes anything from inventory taking of the yacht's selection of fine wines, spirits and general provisioning, to organising laundry and general cleaning. I am also responsible for 12 crews' uniform. Basically, no two days are ever the same.'

Who's who and qualifications required

The qualification structure in the marine industry is not there to create an obstacle in your progress but to create a safe and well-managed environment for you to work in.

The Maritime and Coastguard Agency (MCA) – the executive maritime arm of Department of Transport which is responsible for implementing British and International maritime law and safety policy – administers MCA exams which are required to work on yachts over 200 gt.

The MCA's rules regarding yachts come under the Large Yacht Code or LY2 and are not tonnage based but apply to vessels over 24 m (70 ft). Vessels under 24 m (70 ft) are covered by a different code.

The Royal Yachting Association (RYA), which enforces high standards of marine safety, and the American-based International Yacht Training (IYT), are both accredited by the MCA to run internationally-recognised exams (RYA Yachtmaster and the IYT equivalent – Master of Yachts). Although these RYA and IYT qualifications are necessary as a stepping-stone to the MCA exams, they are also sufficient for Captain and Mate positions working on yachts of up to 200 gt.

The MCA simply accepts the certificates of competency that are issued by the RYA and IYT.

If you have served in the Navy as Petty/Chief Petty Officers or engineers and are looking at entering the yachting industry you may well find you have more than enough to qualify for work aboard a superyacht. For example if you hold a Merchant Navy Second Engineer qualification this will allow you to take a Chief Engineer position on a superyacht.

If you have an aim, therefore, to become a core crew member of a superyacht, it really will pay to focus on obtaining qualifications, spending a year or two working in the yacht charter industry gaining valuable experience, and then approaching the professional superyacht arena.

From the point of view of an owner who has a 44 m hi-tech, luxury cruising yacht – *Salperton* – which has six full time crew and 26 when racing, experience is one of the most important aspects to consider when recruiting staff:

> 'Stability in previous employment is one of the areas we look at, a good personality, plus sailing experience. After all, when there are six crew on an Atlantic crossing for example, you really do need competence at all levels because they are all going to be doing watches. The watch leader would be qualified of course but you still need a stewardess or chef who can stand a watch, so ideally they would have had experience of sailing. When we are sailing or racing, we need them to also be interested, participate and enjoy it.'

Not having any significant qualifications or never having worked on a yacht before doesn't necessarily mean that you are unsuitable for consideration however, because it totally depends on the type of yacht. Captains have been known to recruit crew from a variety of backgrounds such as recent graduates, mechanics, engineers, tour leaders, divers or from the hospitality and hotel sector including even cruise lines. Without relevant qualifications you will, of course, be restricted in some areas, as to how far up the 'ladder' you can climb, but as long as you can prove you have the willingness to learn and have the right work ethic, it's a good way of getting into the industry and gaining solid experience which will put you in a good position in which to base potential future exam training.

One exam that is recommended however, is a basic safety certificate. Percival continued: 'What we advise all crew is they really should consider going and doing their STCW 95 Basic Safety Certificate (more information below) if nothing else. It is not mandatory but most Captains make it a pre-entry requirement. Also, it goes without saying if you have experience and qualifications you'll have a far better chance of gaining employment than someone who just rocks up at the boat asking for a job.'

Annette Corder, 2nd Stewardess on a 52 m (156 ft) motor superyacht, originally worked in investment banking in London for ten years before joining the marine industry with minimal qualifications. Her first job, when she was 40, was working on a classic superyacht with her partner Rob Hickman.

> 'I basically got tired of committing everything to a computer and desk and not seeing the outside world. I wasn't able to see the bigger picture and became very focussed on purely paying my mortgage and not necessarily enjoying what I did, so I decided to quit the rat race with just a Windsurf Level 1 instructor certificate under my belt.

I then did my Yachtmaster and my MCA STCW basic training, and then a four-week cooking course. I know it is great to be qualified but to be honest I think too many tickets [certificates] and no experience can be off-putting to potential employers. You might have been a high flyer in your previous industry but you won't necessarily come in at the top in a new industry so you must be humble. I'd suggest people get the essential tickets they require to get them on their path and then build their experience and go on from there.'

Rob Hickman, Annette's partner who works on the same yacht, as Chief Officer, was another one who decided he wasn't cut out for an office job as software engineer and web developer. He said as a sporty type he found it all very frustrating. Since he's been in the yachting industry he hasn't looked back but does stress that nothing beats experience when looking for a job: 'Although exams for commercial jobs are essential, there is nothing to beat experience, so my advice is to get out there and work as hard as you can. Any other skills you have too are also important. The bigger the boat you go to the more administration is involved, so the more strings you have to your bow the better when it comes to accounting, finance and administration. However, by the time you are in a position to start worrying about those things, you will have enough knowledge behind you already.'

One area worth investigating particularly if you already have the skills is engineering, because engineers are in great demand. This is because the engineering structure is relatively new and there aren't that many people who have the appropriate qualifications says John Percival.

'From my experience of helping candidates through exams, as soon as you get your first level chief engineer certificate you will get a good paying job as an engineer. And if you have experience of two-stroke engines that is a real bonus. A lot of engineers know about diesel engines but struggle when it comes to repairing the yacht toys such as jet skis, which operate two-stroke engines.

We had a female deckhand who, when she was young, used to help her father strip down and rebuild Harley Davidson engines. Not surprisingly, as soon as she arrived in the Med looking for a job on a superyacht, she was snapped up not because she had reams of qualifications but because she was skilled at working with 2-stroke engines.'

Life skills in other areas are also important. Percival says he always recommends students promote themselves with their life skills, adding: 'I found out that one of the lads I'd been

A 36 m sailing yacht like ***Sojana*** **requires a large, professional crew to run it. Photo – Sue Pelling.**

training used to develop 35 mm film in the bath tub at home and he got a job on a very large vessel because of that. He actually ended up being the Captain of it. Even though he was a fairly experienced sailor, it was the fact he used to develop film that got him the job. Apparently the owner of the yacht was a TV cameraman and keen photographer and needed someone to develop his film. So, it just goes to show, qualifications are very important but life skills are everything.'

The more experience you have whether it be sailing, needlework or business, the better chance you'll have of getting on in the industry through transferable skills. Marc Fitzgerald – Captain of the 36 m (100 ft) S/Y *Sojana* – says that there is a definite advantage in having a business background for example, when applying for superyacht jobs. 'Superyachts are small businesses after all, so any experience you have in that field could be valuable. For example, a deckhand with basic bookkeeping skills could find themselves doing the onboard accounts. A stewardess with a nursing or paramedic background could find themselves in charge of medical care.'

Having been fortunate enough to race on *Sojana* in the Caribbean and be invited for dinner onboard I was able to get to know more about how the yacht is run. To my total surprise I learnt that Fitzgerald not only captains the yacht by day but by night – in true Cinderella style – he transforms into the yacht's gourmet chef/waiter. Commenting about how he manages to cope with the two most demanding jobs on the yacht, Fitzgerald said:

> 'I thoroughly enjoy my chef role so I suppose that is the draw. Actually I do believe it is a much harder job to get right than the role of Captain. Interestingly I have no formal cooking qualifications. I have been cooking to a high standard for years, and the owner of *Sojana* was very happy for me to continue to cook for him.
>
> When we chartered *Sojana*, I had some less than happy experiences with career chefs, so eventually decided to raise my game and do it myself. Our charter agents were supportive, but sceptical. After a few very satisfied charterers had given their feedback however, everyone relaxed and let me get on with it.'

The following list of crew positions, job descriptions, salary guide (as published by Superyacht UK), and qualities required for each position should provide an indication of the sort of positions available on a superyacht ranked in no particular hierarchy order. It goes without saying however, the Captain and Officers are the principal positions which hold the most responsibility and therefore demand the biggest salaries.

Captain

A Captain is responsible for the yacht's operation and the safety of everyone on board. It is the ultimate and most desirable job in the superyacht world, but as with all high powered jobs there are certain duties including being at the beck-and-call of the owner and not objecting to being on duty 24 hours a day, seven days a week.

Considerable maritime experience and training for this position will have been gained from working your way up from deck hand, usually on a number of smaller yachts, or from experience gained in the merchant navy.

Skills and attributes required

- Top navigational skills and an understanding of everything about the vessel and its operation.
- An understanding of money management including budget and accountancy on board.

- IT and administration with the ability to deal with authorities on issues such as health and safety.
- A natural leader with good management and decision making skills.
- To be able to manage the upkeep of the vessel including running repairs, yard visits and refit projects.
- The ability to 'host' and entertain.
- Good personnel management skills.
- Being able to deal confidently with people including crew, owners and guests.
- Smart in appearance.
- A desire to act as an ambassador for the ship.

Certification required to become Captain

To work on vessels <200 GT you would need one of the following:
- RYA Yachtmaster Offshore (with Commercial Endorsement).
- RYA Yachtmaster Ocean Certificate of Competence (with Commercial Endorsement).
- IYT Master of Yachts <200 GT.
- MCA STCW Master (Yachts) <200 GT.

To work on vessels <500 GT:
- MCA STCW Master (Yachts) <500 GT Certificate of Competence.

To work on vessels <3000 GT you would need one of the following:
- MCA STCW Master (Yachts) <3000 GT Certificate of Competence.
- MCA Merchant Navy STCW Master <3000 GT.
- MCA STCW Master (Unlimited).

Vessels >3000 GT:
- MCA STCW Master (Unlimited).

Salary guide:
According to surveys carried out by Superyacht UK these are the sort of salaries you can expect to be paid for the captain's position:

- Junior Captain working on a superyacht of <30 metres – £3,500–£5,500 per month.
- More experienced Captain, on superyacht of 30–50 metres – £4,500–£7,000 per month.
- Experienced senior Captain on superyacht >50 metres – £6,000–£10,000 plus per month.

Chief Engineer

Reporting directly to the Captain, the Chief Engineer has overall responsibility for the yacht's engineering department and is ultimately accountable for its safe and efficient operation. It is likely that he/she would have reached this position from an Engineer's position.

As well as being in command, the Chief Engineer's role also includes managing Engineers, Electricians and ETOs (Electronic Technical Officers) and, within his/her daily routine, is in charge of maintaining the mechanical and electrical operations of the yacht, as well as acting as supervisor to ensure the maintenance programme is on schedule.

Also, because many yachts have warranty and/or service contracts for electrical and mechanical equipment carried out by shorebased engineers, the Chief Engineer coordinates operations in this department to ensure the work is carried out efficiently and to standard.

Skills and attributes required

- Technically-minded and versatile with the ability to take on many different roles from working in the engine room to entertaining guests.
- Wide knowledge of yacht systems is required ranging from main engines to yacht accessories such as jet skis, refrigerators, audio and visual equipment, watermakers, generators and air conditioning units.
- An understanding of yachts and the ability to be able to assist on deck particularly in docking, undocking and anchoring operations.
- An ability to manage, supervise and mentor staff in the engine department.
- Experience or an understanding of the International Safety Management (ISM) or Mini ISM.
- Budget, purchasing and sourcing products/equipment.
- Experience and knowledge of onboard IT, and networking systems.

Certification required to become a Chief Engineer (one of the following)

- MCA STCW Chief Engineer (Yachts) certification appropriate for the engine capacity.
- Merchant Navy Second Engineer.
- Chief Engineer certification.
- Merchant Navy certification is required for some larger yachts.

Salary guide

According to surveys carried out by Superyacht UK these are the sort of salaries you can expect to be paid for the Chief Engineer position:

- Depending on size of yacht and experience – between £2,500 and £4,500 per month.
- Larger yachts with more engineering crew to supervise – between £3,800 and £5,500 per month.

First and Second Officer

Most superyachts have a First Officer and most larger yachts employ a Second Officer too in a similar role.

The **First Officer** is the penultimate rank before becoming Captain, which means they are second in command and they are required to have similar qualities as a Captain. This position is sometimes known as the Chief Officer or Chief Mate, and duties include taking charge and overseeing the work of deck crew including Second Officer, Deckhands and Bosuns.

Like the Captain, the main responsibilities of the First Officer include the safety of the yacht, crew and guests. The idea of the First Officer is to set a good example to all crew in not only attitude towards work but also in cleanliness and personal grooming.

They will oversee all deck operations, maintenance, preparation of all equipment on board including yacht accessories such as jet skis, and run safety drills. As well as administrative and safety duties on board, such as implementation of security/port-of-entry paperwork procedures (knowledge of the ISM and ISPS codes), and safe refuelling procedures, the First Officer will take a leading role in navigational passage planning.

The **Second Officer** acts as the First Officer's deputy often with specific responsibility for the navigation, and the upkeep of charts and publications. Other duties include monitoring the navigation and radio equipment and undertaking bridge watches when at sea. The Second Officer may also be the designated security, safety or medical officer.

Skills and attributes required

- Good navigational skills and a firm understanding of the vessel and its operation.
- Good personnel management skills.
- Being able to deal confidently with people including crew, owners and guests and have good customer relation skills.
- Leadership skills with the ability to delegate and assign duties.

Certification required to become a First or Second Officer/Mate (one of the following)

- MCA STCW Officer of the Watch (Yachts) <3,000 gt.
- Chief Mate (Yachts) <3,000 gt certification.

Salary guide

According to surveys carried out by Superyacht UK these are the sort of salaries you can expect to be paid for First and Second Officer positions:

First Officers – between £2,750–£4,000 plus per month
Second Officer – between £2,250–£3,000 per month

Chief Steward and Stewardess

Reporting to the Captain, the Chief Steward/ess is responsible for the comfort and well-being of all the guests on board as well as all aspects of the interior of the yacht. The duties are similar to a Steward/ess but on a more senior level, which means working long hours on a flexible basis and being able to exhibit the ability to serve guests discreetly in a luxury 7-star manner.

As well as providing a first-class hostess service for the guests, the Chief Steward/ess manages and recruits the interior 'house' staff and will have a good working knowledge of the yacht.

Skills and attributes required

- Impeccable attention to detail.
- Cleaning experience, interior maintenance and silver polishing knowledge.
- Table setting skills including napkin folding.
- The ability to think ahead and to anticipate events before they happen.
- Be ready to accept new and varied challenges each day.
- Silver service experience and the ability to coordinate food service.
- Laundry management including ironing.
- An understanding of wines and cocktails and the ability to manage a bar.
- Superb guest service skills.
- Discretion and confidentiality.
- Good interaction skills.
- Team management skills.
- Well-organised and a good administrator, including accounting.
- Multi-lingual.
- Polite and entertaining personality.

Certification required to become a Chief Steward/ess

An MCA STCW Basic Safety Certification is regarded as a pre-requisite for a Chief Steward/ess role although it is not mandatory. However, a background in food and drink, hospitality and catering or customer service would be an advantage when applying for this sort of role. It could also be worth enrolling on a hospitality training programme such as a Steward/ess Certificate accredited by the Professional Yachtsman's Association.

Salary guide

According to surveys carried out by Superyacht UK these are the sort of salaries you can expect to be paid for a Chief Steward/ess position.

Chief Steward/ess – £1,750–£4,000 depending on the size of yacht, and experience.

Chef

The chef aboard *Halcyon* demonstrates how compact the galley work area is likely to be on a classic yacht. Photo – Halcyon Yacht Charter.

On a yacht where entertaining is key, the position of the chef is arguably the most important role. It is also one of the most challenging with responsibilities including the purchase, and transportation of food to the yacht, the preparation and presentation of the food, and the management of the galley (kitchen) including the washing and clearing up to ensure ultimate cleanliness. In a lot of cases, particularly on superyachts at the lower end of the size scale around 24 m (72 ft), it is not unusual for the chef to work alone, but on larger yachts, there may be the assistance of a Sous Chef and possibly a Crew Cook.

The very nature of being on the water means that sometimes it is necessary to adjust to the unstable environment. And, as well as working in the relatively compact confines of a yacht's galley, the Chef has to be adaptable with a range of culinary talents from preparing good, basic, balanced meals to exotic and creative masterpieces. They should also have a good knowledge of fruits, dairy, meats, seafood and other products available only seasonally and perhaps limited by geographical region, as well as being able to cater to those with special dietary requirements, fad diets and food allergies.

Skills and attributes required

- Previous experience as a head or sous chef in a hotel, restaurant or on board other yachts.
- Excellent knowledge of food safety, storage, general health standards, and nutrition.
- Well organised and methodical.
- Management skills.
- Ability to coach those in junior roles and be a good role model.
- Able to plan menus to budget.
- Basic accounting skills.
- Flexible and able to perform gracefully under pressure.
- Able to deliver even on occasions when there is limited availability of produce.
- Adaptable and able to participate in deck duties when there are no guests onboard.
- Interior fire prevention knowledge.
- Hygiene including handling of food and galley cleanliness.
- Ability to stay calm under considerable pressure.
- Good communicator and able to negotiate with suppliers for provisions.

Certification required to become a Head Chef

Although not mandatory most have either recognised qualifications, or have substantial experience working as a chef in hotels or restaurants. However, it is worth obtaining one of the following:

- Level 3 Diploma in Professional Cookery (City and Guilds).
- Level 3 S/NVQ Professional Cookery (City and Guilds).
- Other industry-recognised international qualifications.

Plus:

- MCA STCW Basic Safety Certification.

Salary guide

According to surveys carried out by Superyacht UK these are the sort of salaries you can expect to be paid as a Chef:

Chef (entry level) – £1,750–£2,250 per month
Chef (with experience) – £2,500–£4,000 per month
Chefs (high profile) – upwards of £5,000 per month

Engineer

The Engineer answers directly to the Chief Engineer and, as well being an expert on all the main mechanical functions and electrical operations (and electrical maintenance) on the yacht, the Engineer – just like the Chief Engineer – should be good at administration, have managerial and communication skills, and be capable of adapting to a variety of jobs including interacting with guests.

Being able to troubleshoot and repair, and having a good knowledge base of sourcing and purchasing yacht parts, are some of the other main qualities required for position as Engineer.

Skills and attributes required

- Technically-minded and versatile with the ability to take on many different roles from working in the engine room to entertaining guests.
- Wide knowledge of yacht systems is required ranging from main engines to fixing refrigerators, audio and visual equipment, watermakers, generators and air conditioning units.
- An understanding of yachts and the ability to assist on deck particularly in docking, undocking and anchoring operations.
- An ability to mentor staff in junior engineering roles.

Certification required to become an Engineer (one of the following)

- MCA STCW Basic Safety certification.
- Merchant Navy or Royal Navy Engine Room Watch Keeping Certificate or equivalent.

Salary guide

According to surveys carried out by Superyacht UK these are the sort of salaries you can expect to be paid for an Engineer position:

Engineer – depending on size of yacht and experience – £2,000–£3,500 per month.
Engineer with over five years experience – £2,800–£4,000 plus per month.

Assistant Engineer

A junior, entry-level position to provide a good apprenticeship in learning how a superyacht engineering department runs.

Salary guide

According to surveys carried out by Superyacht UK this is the sort of salary you can expect to be paid for an Assistant Engineer position:

Assistant Engineer – £1,500 per month

Electronic Technical Officer (ETO)

The ETO, who reports to the Chief Engineer, is responsible for the day-to-day maintenance and wellbeing of all things technical on large (over 60 m [180 ft]) superyachts.

The significance of hi-tech communications and entertainment means that the role of an ETO is becoming more important, with jobs ranging from IT (information technology) and AV (audiovisual) to Global Maritime Distress Safety System (GMDSS) and radar.

Because technology is evolving so fast, and owners of superyachts generally have a desire to be able to impress their guests with the latest hi-tech equipment such as television and music systems, it is important the ETO is well ahead of the game when it comes to researching, sourcing and installing new equipment.

Skills and attributes required

- Highly technical person who is as good at troubleshooting as he/she is at fixing problems.
- An awareness of urgency and the ability to remain calm when the pressure is on.
- A thorough understanding of yacht systems.
- The ability to work alone in a fairly isolated environment.

Certification required to become an ETO

- MCA STCW Basic Safety certification.
- Electrics/electronics qualifications would be an advantage although not mandatory.
- MCA STCW Engineering certification may also be a requirement, depending on the yacht.

Salary guide

According to surveys carried out by Superyacht UK this is the sort of salary you can expect to be paid for a position as ETO:

ETO – depending on experience – £2,000–£3,500 per month

Second/Sous Chef

A Second Chef is the Sous Chef, who is second in command in the galley and works alongside the Chef on larger superyachts.

As well as meal planning and assisting the chef, and having a firm grip on budget, purchasing, equipment, food preparation and storage, the second chef is generally responsible for the planning, preparation and production of crew meals. It is a highly challenging position but a good choice for anyone who aspires to work their way up to become a professional yacht chef.

As is the case with the Chief Chef, the very nature of being on the water means it is sometimes necessary to adjust to the unstable environment and adapt to working in the relatively compact confines of a yacht's galley.

Skills and attributes required

- Previous cook/restaurant experience is essential.
- Excellent knowledge of food, safety, storage, general health standards, and nutrition and able to cater to those with special dietary requirements, fad diets and food allergies.
- Flexible and able to perform gracefully under pressure.
- Well organised and methodical.
- Able to plan menus to budget.

- Able to deliver even on occasions when there is limited availability of produce.
- Interior fire prevention knowledge.
- Hygiene including handling of food and galley cleanliness.
- Ability to stay calm under considerable pressure.
- Good communicator and able to negotiate with suppliers for provisions.

Certification required to become Second/Sous Chef

Although it is not mandatory, one of the recognised qualifications listed below would be an advantage. Plus many employers require a candidate to hold an MCA STCW Basic Safety Certificate.

- Level 3 Diploma in Professional Cookery (City and Guilds).
- Level 3 S/NVQ Professional Cookery (City and Guilds).

Salary guide

According to surveys carried out by Superyacht UK this is the sort of salary you can expect to be paid for a position as a Second/Sous Chef:

- Second/Sous Chef (starting) – £1,500–£2,500 per month.
- Second/Sous Chef (with previous superyacht experience) – £2,000–£3,000 per month.

Stew-Cook

On smaller yachts in the 24 m (72 ft) range, it is not unusual to find employment as a Stew-Cook or a Stew-Chef. It is basically the cook and steward/ess position funnelled into one job. These jobs also tend to be much less formal and more relaxed than similar positions on larger yachts but don't be fooled into thinking they are any less challenging. In fact, with the responsibilities of two jobs you'll find your feet will never touch the ground.

Daily duties for this position are likely to include cleaning, ironing and washing laundry, sourcing and shopping for produce, preparing, cooking and serving food.

Skills and attributes required

- Previous cook/restaurant experience is essential.
- Excellent knowledge of food, safety, storage, general health standards, and nutrition and able to cater to those with special dietary requirements, fad diets and food allergies.
- Ability to learn quickly and stay calm under pressure.
- Cleaning experience.
- Table setting skills including napkin folding.
- Be ready to accept new and varied challenges each day.
- Laundry management including ironing.
- Well-organised.
- Adaptable to different working environments and conditions.
- Budget management.

Certification required to become a Stew-Chef

Although it is not mandatory, one of the recognised qualifications listed below would be an advantage. Plus many employers require a candidate to hold an MCA STCW Basic Safety Certificate.

- Level 3 Diploma in Professional Cookery (City and Guilds).
- Level 3 S/NVQ Professional Cookery (City and Guilds).

Salary guide

According to surveys carried out by Superyacht UK this is the sort of salary you can expect to be paid for a position as a Stew-Cook:

- Stew Cook (starting) – £1,500–£2,500 per month.
- Stew-Cook (with previous superyacht experience) – £2,000–£3,000 per month.

Bosun

The stowage and maintenance of yacht tenders is part of a deckhand's daily routine. Photo – Camper & Nicholsons International.

The Bosun, sometimes known as the Senior Deckhand, and who answers to the Captain, is responsible for the maintenance and exterior cleanliness of the yacht. The role also involves managing the deck hands, and all deck operations including the use, maintenance and stowage of yacht tenders and equipment, and mooring lines.

On wooden, classic yachts in particular, an understanding of wood preparation, paints and varnishes and how to apply them flawlessly, is essential. Knowledge of caulking (stopping up the cracks and gaps on wood deck) and glassfibre repair would also be an asset.

The Bosun will often oversee the embarking and disembarking of guests, and in a security role will ensure only those with valid authorisation are allowed on board the yacht.

Because the Bosun will invariably spend a lot of time with guests or owners, the working hours in this sort of job are likely to be long and flexible.

Skills and attributes required

- A positive attitude and a keen eye for detail and service.
- A background in yachting, and ideally experience as a deckhand.
- A good understanding of exterior and general deck duties on a luxury yacht.
- Ability to delegate duties and work assignments to deckhands.
- Capable tender driver.
- Works well within a team.
- Basic engineering knowledge.

Certification required to become a Bosun

There are no mandatory requirements for certification or qualifications to become a Bosun but it would be an advantage to have the following:

- MCA Yacht Rating Certificate.
- RYA Power Boat level 2 or IYT Tender Driver Licence.
- GMDSS VHF/SRC Radio Operators Certificate.
- RYA Yachtmaster Offshore or IYT Master of Yachts <200 gt.
- MCA STCW Master (Yachts) <200 gt or STCW OOW (Yachts) Certification.
- MCA STCW Basic Safety Certificate (often considered essential).

Salary guide

According to surveys carried out by Superyacht UK this is the sort of salary you can expect to be paid for a position as a Bosun

Bosun (entry level) – £2,500 and £3,500 per month
Bosun (with experience on larger yachts) – £4,000 per month

Deckhand

Newcomers to the superyacht industry will probably find that a Deckhand is one of the most sensible entry-level jobs to apply for. As long as you are willing to work hard, this is the job where you'll learn the most about the general operations aboard a superyacht. Even if you have qualifications above this role, a stint as a deckhand will put you in a better position and give you so much more confidence about what you are capable of.

Depending on the size of the yacht, you'll either be working alone or together with up to five other deckhands. It is a job of many roles but the main responsibility of a deckhand is the exterior maintenance of the yacht and the ability to keep it in pristine condition at all times. This includes cleaning, painting/varnishing, polishing, sanding, restoration, glassfibre repairs, carpentry, mooring line handling, driving tenders, accompanying guests when using yacht sports equipment, diving (if qualified), assisting cabin staff with serving meals, cleaning cabins or even helping out the chef in the galley.

Skills and attributes required

- Basic seafaring knowledge.
- Experience of navigation, boat handling, engines and radio equipment.
- Not afraid of hard work.
- Positive attitude.
- Willing to learn on the job.
- Ability to take direction.
- Professional, smart appearance.
- Good teamworker.

Certification required to become a Deckhand

There are no mandatory requirements for certification or qualifications to become a deckhand, experience is generally more important, however, it would be an advantage to have at least a STCW 95 Basic Training Certificate and any of the following:

- RYA Day Skipper.
- RYA Power Boat Level 2.
- VHF/SRC Radio Operators Certificate.
- IYT Tender Driving Licence.

Salary guide

According to surveys carried out by Superyacht UK this is the sort of salary you can expect to be paid for a position as a deckhand:

Deckhand (entry level) – £1,250–£1,750 per month.
Deckhand (experienced) – £1,750–£2,000 per month.

Support jobs

As well as the above key crew jobs there are plenty of support jobs that run alongside the superyacht industry including, financial controllers, dive master/instructor, helicopter pilot/mechanic, spa/beauty therapist, nanny, medic/nurse or fishing specialist.

The list goes on but if you are keen on ensuring you get to spend as much time on the water as possible actively sailing the boat, you need to be aware that becoming a core member of the crew such as captain, first mate, first officer, are the sort of jobs you should be looking at. Some of the support type jobs are shorebased which means time spent at sea could be limited.

Training

Assuming you decide to take the professional approach and get yourself qualified, you'll need to formulate a plan to make the process as sustainable as possible. Whatever route you take, whether it is a 'fast track' or more conventional way of obtaining relevant qualifications for the job you choose, there is a large time factor involved. Be aware also, that the training is also going to be relatively costly which, together with the cost of living while you are effectively out of work, will make a large dent in your new career budget.

And remember, even if you are newly qualified, you are unlikely to be able to step into a key role aboard a superyacht without previous experience. Therefore, make sure you allow plenty of time within your plan to obtain the skills necessary for your particular dream role.

There are training centres all over the UK specialising in RYA and MCA qualifications for superyacht employment. Most of these centres, including the UKSA (United Kingdom Sailing Academy) based in Cowes, Isle of Wight, and Hoylake Sailing School Ltd, on the Wirral, Cheshire will be only too happy to chat about your career ideas and advise on which would be the best qualification route to take. They will also be able to advise on cost of training which you'll find will vary according to what is included, such as exam fees or whether the course is residential. Another interesting source of information if you are serious about seeking work in the superyacht industry, is superyachtuk.com – the website of the superyacht arm of the British Marine Federation – which has a useful career section.

Marc Fitzgerald – Captain of the 36 m (115 ft) S/Y *Sojana* says having sailing and seamanship experience and continually improving your skills seems like blindingly obvious advice.

> Certain qualifications are necessary, but there is no substitute for skill and experience. If you want to clock up some good experience, my advice is to sign up for some yacht racing as this is a great way of fast-tracking skills because it is relatively intense and demanding. Yacht delivery is also a good training ground, as you will be part of a small crew, with commercial pressure to get from A to B in one piece, as quickly as possible. Polishing brass on a superyacht tied to the dock however, is not really going to prepare you for much.

As far as courses and training are concerned Fitzgerald, who has his MCA Class IV certificate, says he regrets his lack of knowledge of CAD software and wishes he'd had the time to learn more about that. 'I wish I had the training and the time to become competent with CAD software. Most designers and engineers have finite patience when it comes to deciphering clumsy pencil sketches on a scrap of paper.'

Commitment

The ability of being able to commit yourself to a life 'at sea' in the superyacht world is a huge consideration. The idea of all the glitz and glamour associated with working on some of the most expensive yachts in the world for the rich and famous and earning huge amounts of money may sound idyllic but in reality it is in the service industry and can be one of the most demanding and challenging careers you're ever likely to find. Whether you are the cleaner or the captain you are providing a service and are at the beck and call of the owners at all times.

It can also be one of most lonely careers because the amount of time you have to spend away from home means you'll have to make the stark choice between family and loved ones, or sailing.

Having said that, there is movement afoot to introduce more flexible conditions. Because owners, captains and managers are now beginning to recognise that salary does not necessarily guarantee the retention of good crew, a leave rotation system is gradually being initiated and promoted in order to secure professional crew.

While there is no getting away from the fact that long stints away from home are the nature of the job, this new system should make having a family life slightly more possible.

Superyacht crews tend to sign up for a 12-month contract with six-week leave at the end of 12 months. Rotation is where you do three months on the vessel and three months off which is effectively a job share. Sometimes you will even find there are three people covering two jobs – three months on and two months off, or similar.

Captain Percival commenting on job rotation said: 'It is a fantastic idea. Because superyachting has become a career with a professional structure, job longevity has increased substantially. A crew used to last a couple of years in the same job but it is now five and a half to six years. You'll even find there are guys whose boats are berthed in the Med the whole winter every year, who live somewhere in the Med so they can have a family life too.'

Family man Marc Fitzgerald – Captain of the 36 m (115 ft) S/Y *Sojana* – spoke to me about the ability to juggle a superyacht career with family life, and confessed to having averaged just seven nights a year home in Gurnard since 2004:

> 'I was lucky that my son's pre-school years coincided with the design process and build of *Sojana* which meant I was largely based at home, in Cowes on the Isle of Wight. Prior to Lewis and Euans' birth however, I was away or at sea for 9 months in every 12. When my daughter Ellise was born in 1995, we were preparing for the Rolex Transat from NY to Cowes, so I flew home for the birth, then straight back and off to sea . . . Now the whole family moves to Antigua for the winter season, so we have a good family life there.'

Life on board

Whatever job you choose aboard a yacht, you'll probably find you'll get a dose of 'cabin fever' at some point during your career. By the very nature of the job you'll be working in a relatively small space with a small group of colleagues for sometimes weeks/months on end. Living conditions can also be fairly cramped particularly during charter periods where all cabins are utilised for guests, which means you'll probably be crammed in a cubbyhole and have little privacy.

Having the right personality to live a life on the high seas therefore is one of the most important factors and should be a big consideration. Duncan Abel who worked as a skipper and mate aboard a variety of sailing superyachts after his early career in the Royal Marines, said it is important to be outgoing, bright, sociable and hard working, and have the ability to learn new skills, be adaptable, and be willing to work as a team member: 'Remember, it's not all fun and frolics, there's a lot of hard work like dealing with very demanding people who expect to have what they want.'

Annette Corder – second stewardess on a 52 m (156 ft) motoryacht – worked in investment banking in London for 10 years before she joined the marine industry and said that as well as a sense of humour you need to be efficient, well organised and self motivated. 'My advice for anyone considering this sort of work is, not to go in thinking you know everything. Be humble and see how the boat runs. Keep your head down and do your job to the best of your ability.'

Marc Fitzgerald – Captain of the 36 m (115 ft) S/Y *Sojana* – said that privacy, or lack of it, it is one of the most difficult things to come to terms with: 'Having spent my whole working life in cramped quarters, I can happily plug in the iPod, or read a book, and tune out the world, but some people can never adjust to living on top of one another. It can be a bit of a "Big Brother" pressure cooker, nightmare experience for some, many of whom decide they are not cut out for that sort of life.'

Spending your life working at sea does carry inherent risks, so it is important to understand the relevance of safety at sea, and to have a respect for the elements. There will be times when you'll have concerns about the conditions particularly when the wind is strong (over 30 kts) and the waves create uncomfortable conditions onboard.

Seasickness is also something to be aware of because it can strike anyone at any time regardless of the amount of previous sailing experience. It is one of the most debilitating and extremely uncomfortable conditions you are likely to experience but in most cases you *will* acclimatise.

Rough conditions at sea can sometimes take their toll and in worse case scenarios, result in emergency situations. Captain Marc Fitzgerald who's been working on yachts for many years says you have to be aware and know the procedure just in case there is an emergency situation:

> 'We did have an incident on *Sojana* during a transatlantic race when a crew member broke his arm very badly. We set the arm on board, then turned around and headed for the nearest hospital in St Pierre et Miquelon, a French colony in Newfoundland. After racing over the Grand Banks in thick fog and 20 knots of wind, we arrived in fog so thick we could not make out where the harbour walls were as we entered using radar. Our man was rushed to hospital, but after an x-ray proved the severity of the break, he was flown to Quebec for surgery involving a lot of titanium plates and screws. It was back to the race for us, and more horrible weather. I think I ran on pure adrenalin for a few days. Also, retrieving a man overboard in a gale also gave me nightmares for a while.'

Where to look for jobs

Once you've had a chance to think about the options and decide whether you want to use your current qualifications (if you already have them), investigate training opportunities, or just head out there armed with 'life skills' only, it's worth taking a look at some of the many yacht crew agency websites to see the sort of jobs available and salaries being offered. A good resource is www.jf-recruiting.com, which lists many of the key agencies such as www.dovaston.com, which is a leading agency for the placement of professional crew. As mentioned earlier in the chapter, you'll find the motor yacht jobs (M/Y) far exceed the number of sailing yacht (S/Y) jobs but it will give you plenty of ideas to ponder with.

Some websites request information such as CV. Always be aware, however, about imparting too much information, and make sure you get to know the company and have a firm idea of what sort of job you are looking for before you advertise your skills online.

The old adage: 'it's not what you know but who you know' is probably one of the most useful things to remember when seeking a job in the marine industry. It really does pay to network and get to know who's who. Mike French – President of International Yacht Training – Fort Lauderdale says taking day work/part time jobs around the dock really does get your name known. 'Dockwalking and handing out your resumes at events such as boatshows and, charter shows are some of the best ways to promote yourself, but training companies – the place where you train for your qualifications – are among the best places to help you find a job.'

Rob Hickman Chief Officer of a 52 m (156 ft) superyacht endorsed this advice adding:

> 'Until you have been in the industry a number of years and have established yourself, people won't be knocking down your door to employ you, however good you think you are.
>
> My advice is to get out there, swallow your pride, and use the agents, do the dock-walk and promote yourself in the best possible light because you can guarantee there are plenty of guys trying hard right behind you.'

Working as a couple

Partners Rob Hickman and Annette Corder have been working together on superyachts for over six years. They spent many enjoyable years working on a British, privately owned sailing superyacht but now work on a 52 m (156 ft) motor superyacht based in the Western Mediterranean. Rob is Chief Officer and Annette Corder is 2nd Stewardess.

Hickman chatting about the opportunities available to couples:

> 'I think if you can present yourselves as an established and professional couple there's a high chance you'll be offered a good job. When looking for work we are open to the fact that we might not be able to get something together, so we always consider ourselves lucky when it works out. It's probably one of the most idyllic jobs for us because during our time on yachts we have barely spent time away from each other.'

As far as privacy goes Rob says they couldn't ask for more: 'We have a cabin together with a bunk, en suite shower with limitless supplies of hot water, TV and internet facilities. Coming from a sailing yacht it all seems very extravagant for crew.'

While there are many couples like Rob and Annette who enjoy working together as a successful partnership, it pays to be aware of the problems that could occur should the personal side of a partnership dissolve.

Visas

When looking for a job bear in mind you'll probably need a visa. Visa issues are incredibly complex so if you are intending to get a job abroad or work on a yacht that cruises

Rob Hickman and Annette Corder have been working successfully together on superyachts for over six years. Photo – Halcyon Yacht Charter.

extensively, you'll need to do a lot of research to find out the procedure you should take to obtain a visa.

Mike French – President of International Yacht Training – Fort Lauderdale says getting the appropriate visas and understanding what you need is a very important aspect of working abroad. 'In the United States of America for example, unless you have a B1/B2 visa, which allows you to enter the US aboard a yacht, you'll be sent home. Even then if you come to the US on a B1/B2 visa and say "I am looking for a job", they'll throw you out. You are actually not looking for a job; you're hoping to get employed as a crewmember on a privately registered yacht. It is a very difference sentence.'

Because there are few, if any, places that sum up exactly what is required, it is important to carry out thorough research including looking at websites such as dockwalk.com and thecrewreport.com. These websites for the professional yachting industry are useful resources with their forums allowing you to connect with other crewmembers who may have already been through similar experiences and could offer advice.

Tax reminder

If you are a British Citizen working on a yacht in the EU, it pays to be aware that you are still liable to pay tax in this country. If in any doubt about your tax liabilities, contact HM Revenue & Customs or go to: www.hmrc.gov.uk for more help, or track down a Seafarer's Tax specialist.

Chapter 4
Teaching and coaching

Teaching sailing can be one of the most rewarding jobs in the marine industry, and offers a wealth of opportunities in both the UK and abroad once you've qualified. From teaching youngsters on the Solent or disabled sailors in Londons Docklands, to coaching a professional racing team in the Mediterranean, the opportunities are vast. Teaching is also one of the most structured routes to take because, thanks to the Royal Yachting Association's (RYA) defined and well-constructed teaching programmes in the UK, which cover all aspects of sailing, motorboating and windsurfing, there is plenty of choice in which to specialise.

Because in Great Britain alone there is over 7,000 miles of coastline, and thousands of miles of inland waterways, lakes and reservoirs, which provide opportunities to take to the water, teaching others to get afloat is certainly worth considering. In their research, the British Marine Federation claims that 2.9 million adults from the UK took part in boating activities in 2010 which means many of these will have participated at RYA recognised training centres.

Teaching sailing can be one of the most rewarding jobs in the marine industry. Photo – Sunsail.

There are over 20,000 RYA qualified instructors worldwide working in all areas of the industry, and with over 2,300 RYA recognised training establishments including shorebased centres around the globe, there are plenty of job opportunities.

It is also possible to teach informally, more in the role of a charter skipper who provides instruction. See the section on setting up a charter school and remember the importance of being properly insured.

You do however, need to possess certain qualities to be able to teach, which include being a good communicator. Being sure that teaching is your true vocation in life, and having a passion to pass on your experience and knowledge to others must also be priorities to consider.

The following qualities are important if you are thinking about teaching sailing, or you want to transform yourself from a good sailing teacher to a great sailing teacher:

- Empathetic – the ability to bond with your students, to understand their feelings and difficulties.
- Inspirational – to help others find their skills and abilities and never see anyone as a lost cause.
- Positive – to see the positive side of things and keep a smile on your face even when the going gets tough. The ability to keep calm is also essential.
- Confidence – believing in yourself and not taking upsets too personally.
- Voice projection – learn how to throw your voice and speak with authority because you need your students to be able to understand what you are saying when you are instructing from a training support boat.
- Open minded – to be able to acknowledge new ideas and new approaches, and be willing to listen to others' ideas. Acknowledging the fact that however much you know, you'll never stop learning, so being willing to learn from your peers and your students is imperative.
- Creative – having a creative flair and being able to have a unique approach to teaching can prove motivational and positive.
- Role model – being able to set a good example at all times.
- Sense of humour – having a sense of humour certainly helps and can create a positive atmosphere by lowering the barriers.
- Presentation skills – having the ability to deliver good, clear, concise instructions and be passionate about what you are teaching.

As with all specialist sports, having the experience and ability to teach others is an important factor, but with sailing you don't have to have spent a lifetime on the water to be good enough to teach. In fact – although it's not a particularly wise option – you could, in theory take a zero-to-hero style, fast track commercially endorsed Yachtmaster course, progress from a novice to teaching people how to sail on a 20 m (60 ft) yacht in little more than four months. The chances of an employer taking you on and letting you loose with his yacht in charge of a group of novices with such little experience however, are fairly slim, but according to Simon Jinks – former RYA Chief Cruising Coach – you have to take each case individually.

'I understand why fast-track courses are sometimes frowned upon; I for one used to really hate the idea of them, but having been very much involved, I now have a different opinion. Some of these sailors are very good and where they come from doesn't really matter. If you think about it, these sailors have done 15 weeks at sea which is a lot. They either take to it and they are pretty good, or they are not. It is as simple as that. And whether they have been doing it for 20 years or just 20 weeks full time, it doesn't matter. It depends on their ability, and that you can tell almost immediately.'

Thirty-six-year-old Jim Prendergast is a Chief Instructor at Ondeck – one of the largest global RYA training and corporate hospitality/events companies, based in the UK. But like many who progress into the marine industry Prendergast worked as a high flyer in the City of London. He decided to quit his well-paid job working in investor relations when he was 27 years old and take up a new career in the sailing world. Because he needed to progress fairly rapidly he took a fast-track course and gained his RYA sailing qualifications. Within ten years Prendergast had progressed to a top position on the teaching ladder. Talking about his decision to change careers, Prendergast said: 'I remember the company I worked for being bought by an American company and I couldn't really see myself wanting to stay there so I basically resigned on the Monday, which was just two days after the takeover announcement. I surprised myself as much as anyone. I gave up a very good job with an excellent salary and headed into the unknown. What pushed me, I suppose, was the fact I was still young, and had no dependents, so really it was the perfect time – a now or never situation.'

And over a decade on, does Prendergast feel it was the right move? 'I have never regretted my decision although there's no getting away from the fact that sailing can be very tough and demanding, and occasionally you are away from home for a long period of time.'

Although Prendergast wasn't totally new to sailing when he joined the industry he had to go about getting qualifications. 'I made the most of my gardening leave by signing up for a fast track course and got my qualifications. This allowed me to carry out a few yacht delivery jobs before going into teaching. I am now a full time instructor and have my RYA Yachtmaster Ocean certificate.'

So what are the qualifications you need to teach sailing?

To start with you need qualifications within the area in which you want to specialise and, as a rule of thumb, you'll find you won't be able to teach above the qualifications you already hold. Here's a guide of the type of RYA courses available.

This information, sourced from the Royal Yachting Association, will hopefully provide you with an idea of the sort of teaching you may want to pursue.

You'll need to be qualified before you can take out a yacht full of clients. Photo – Sunsail.

Yacht instructors

Cruising Instructor (CI)

The first step in teaching sailing on yachts within the RYA scheme is to become qualified as a Cruising Instructor, before moving up to the Yachtmaster Instructor qualification.

Cruising Instructors are able to teach up to the level of the Day Skipper practical course through an RYA recognised training centre. The course can be taken in either sail or motor cruisers, and your certificate will be endorsed accordingly.

Eligibility

- Yachtmaster Offshore Certificate of Competence.
- First Aid certificate.
- Commercial endorsement.
- Basic sea survival certificates.
- Medical fitness examination (ML5, ENG1 or medical issued by a National Maritime Authority).

Validity The Cruising Instructor qualification is valid for five years. After five years you must either be re-assessed or, preferably, progress to the Yachtmaster Instructor course.

Yachtmaster Instructor (YMI)
Yachtmaster Instructors are able to teach all practical courses within the RYA Cruising Scheme through an RYA recognised training centre.

The course can be taken in either sail or motor cruisers, and your certificate will be endorsed accordingly.

Eligibility
- Yachtmaster Offshore Certificate of Competence.
- First Aid certificate.
- Commercial endorsement.
- Basic sea survival certificate.
- Medical fitness examination (ML5, ENG1 or medical issued by a National Maritime Authority).
- Cruising Instructor certificate.
- More than 7,000 miles experience.

Validity The Yachtmaster Instructor qualification is valid for up to five years, at the RYA's discretion. Candidates must attend a two-day updating course at least every five years to retain their qualifications.

Probationary courses Instructors who have passed their qualifying course must satisfactorily run two RYA practical courses at a recognised centre within 12 months of the qualifying course. Following this the Instructor qualification may be awarded.

Dinghy, Keelboat and Multihull Instructors

This scheme is for anyone wanting to teach sailing in dinghies, small keelboats and multihulls, and as with all RYA schemes, it is progressive which means you can develop your skills and qualifications by taking endorsement courses, working towards Senior Instructor level or, ultimately, becoming a Coach/Assessor.

Assistant Instructor (AI)
The Assistant Instructor is a competent small boat sailor who has been trained to assist instructors in teaching sailing up to the standard of the RYA Level 2 or Stage 3 courses. They must work under the supervision of an RYA senior instructor (SI) or the Chief Instructor of a keelboat training centre.

As the AI's training is limited to assisting qualified instructors and does not include first aid or powerboat handling, AIs will always be working under direct supervision.

Eligibility Candidates must hold one of the RYA Sailing Scheme advanced modules and have the recommendation of their centre's Principal.

Certificate Validity The AI certificate is valid only at that centre for five years.

Dinghy, Keelboat or Multihull Instructor

Instructors teaching the National Sailing Scheme need to be qualified for the type of boat in which they teach, such as dinghies, small keelboats or multihulls.

In addition the instructor certificate is endorsed to show whether you are qualified to teach on inland or coastal waters.

Qualities The instructor should be a competent, experienced sailor capable of sailing a training boat in strong winds and handling small powerboats. The instructor has been assessed as competent to teach adults and children, beginners and improvers.

Although responsible for teaching individuals and small groups, the instructor has not been assessed as competent in running a sailing centre, and should always work under the supervision of an RYA Senior instructor (for dinghy and multihull courses) or the chief instructor of a keelboat training centre.

Eligibility

- Minimum age 16.
- Valid first aid certificate.
- RYA Powerboat Level 2 certificate.
- Pre-entry sailing assessment completed within one year prior to the instructor training course.

Pre-entry assessment During the assessment the candidate will be asked to complete the following:

- Sail around a triangular course of 100 m (minimum) legs to the best of their ability using all the boat's normal equipment, including spinnaker if carried.
- Sail a tight circular course around a stationary boat, making only one tack and one gybe.
- Sail a 'follow my leader' course behind another boat. The course may include all points of sailing and may be behind another sailing dinghy or behind a powered boat.
- Pick up a man overboard dummy; the boat to be stopped and more than one attempt should not be needed.

Candidates may also be asked to complete some of the following:

- Sail without a rudder, or with the tiller on a loose elastic, around a triangular course. Candidate will be expected to make good progress around the course in a seamanlike manner (not applicable to keelboat or multihull instructor candidates).

- Lee shore landing and launching.
- Anchor or pick up a mooring – wind against tidal flow.
- Come alongside a moored boat – wind against tidal flow.
- Recover a capsized dinghy and sail away (not keelboats).

Certificate validity Instructor certificates are valid for five years from the date of issue, provided that a valid first aid certificate is maintained.

Keelboat/Multihull endorsements

Candidates who complete their instructor course in dinghies, but who want to teach in small keelboats or multihulls should obtain the relevant endorsement. Endorsement courses are run over two days by Coach/Assessors with the relevant experience and who have been appointed by the RYA.

Advanced instructor

The advanced instructor is an instructor with a wide background of sailing experience who has been trained to teach the Performance Sailing and Sailing with Spinnakers courses.

Eligibility

- RYA Instructor certificate, and will usually have recorded at least one season's experience of teaching sailing since qualifying.
- Skilled to at least the level of the Performance Sailing and Sailing with Spinnakers courses.
- Powerboat handling experience in a teaching environment.

Racing Instructor

The endorsement to become a Racing Instructor should be obtained by instructors with experience of club racing who wish to teach racing skills.

Eligibility

- Dinghy instructor trainees who have experience of club racing (minimum completed nine races and assistant race officer role once) may qualify during their instructor training course. Alternatively qualified dinghy instructors may undertake further training at a later date with a Coach/Assessor.

Senior Instructor (SI)

The Senior Instructor is an experienced instructor who has been assessed as competent to organise and manage courses within the RYA's Sailing Scheme. They are qualified to organise and control group sailing tuition and to supervise and assist instructors.

SIs must be confident, and competent managers, capable of organising groups of all ages and directing the work of their instructors.

A RYA recognised dinghy/keelboat/multihull training centre must have a current SI as its Principal or Chief Sailing Instructor, though a Yachtmaster instructor may fulfil this role in a keelboat centre.

Eligibility

- RYA Dinghy Instructor certificate.
- Minimum age 18.
- Two years intermittent, or one year full time dinghy instructing experience since qualifying.
- RYA Safety Boat certificate.
- Valid first aid certificate.
- Signed recommendation from the Principal of an RYA training centre.

Windsurfing

Qualifying to become a windsurfing instructor will provide plenty of opportunities for a job in the sun. Photo – Minorca Sailing.

Windsurfing Assistant Instructor (AI)

The Assistant Instructor is a competent intermediate who has been trained to assist instructors in teaching windsurfing up to the standard of Youth Stage 1 and Adult Start Windsurfing courses. They must work under the supervision of a RYA senior instructor (SI).

Eligibility

- RYA Windsurfing Scheme Intermediate non-planing certificate, and have the recommendation of their centre's Principal.

Certificate validity The AI certificate is valid only at that centre for five years.

Start Windsurfing Instructor

RYA Start Windsurfing instructors are qualified to teach the Start Windsurfing course and Stages 1 and 2 of the Youth Windsurfing Scheme under the supervision of a senior instructor.

Eligibility

- Minimum age 16.
- Intermediate non-planing certificate with beach starting and non-planing gybe clinics.
- RYA Powerboat Level 2 certificate.
- Valid first aid qualification.

Intermediate windsurfing instructor

RYA Intermediate windsurfing instructors are qualified to teach the Intermediate course and Youth Windsurfing Scheme under the supervision of a senior instructor.

Eligibility

The prerequisites for the Intermediate Non-planing Instructor

- Minimum age 16.
- Start windsurfing instructor.
- Intermediate certificate plus beach starting and non-planing carve gybe clinics.
- RYA Powerboat Level 2 certificate.
- Valid first aid certificate.
- Evidence of 50 hours logged as a Start Windsurfing Instructor.

The prerequisites for the Intermediate Planing Instructor

- Minimum age 16.
- Start windsurfing/Intermediate Non-planing Instructor.
- Advanced certificate with waterstart and carve gybe clinics.
- RYA Powerboat Level 2 certificate.
- Valid first aid certificate.
- Evidence of 50 hours logged as a Start Windsurfing or Intermediate Non-planing Instructor.

Windsurfing advanced instructor

RYA advanced windsurfing instructors are qualified to teach the Advanced course and all stages of the Youth Windsurfing Scheme under the supervision of a Senior Instructor.

Eligibility

- Intermediate Planing Instructor certificate.
- Minimum age 18.
- Minimum of a competent Advanced Windsurfing certificate holder plus clinics in water starting and carve gybing.
- RYA Powerboat Level 2 certificate.
- Valid first aid qualification.
- Evidence of 100 hours logged as an Intermediate Planing instructor.

Windsurfing Senior Instructor (SI)

The Senior Instructor is an experienced instructor who has been assessed as competent to organise and manage courses within the RYA's Windsurfing Scheme. They are qualified to organise and control group windsurfing tuition and to supervise and assist instructors.

A RYA recognised windsurfing training centre must have a current SI as its Principal or chief windsurfing instructor.

Qualities of a Senior Instructor

- A safe teacher; working within a known environment, a good leader, capable of working to a high level within any teaching establishment almost seeing problems before they occur.
- SIs must also have the objectivity required for conducting assessments and the interpersonal skills needed to debrief unsuccessful students effectively and tactfully in a good manner.

Eligibility

- RYA Start Windsurfing Instructor certificate.
- Minimum age 18.
- Evidence of two seasons full-time instructing as an RYA Windsurfing Start Instructor.
- Recommendation by a Principal of a Recognised Training Centre.
- A valid first aid qualification.
- RYA Safety boat certificate.

Windsurfing Racing Instructor

RYA Racing Instructors are qualified to teach the RYA Start Racing course under the supervision of a Senior Instructor.

Eligibility

- Start Windsurfing Instructor (or above).
- Minimum age 16.

- RYA Powerboat Level 2 certificate.
- Valid first aid certificate.

Racing Coach Level 2

This course is the next step, and teaches the techniques that provide windsurfers with basic skills involved with racing.

Eligibility

- A valid first aid qualification such as RYA's First Aid Certificate, First Aid at Work, First Aid at Sea, or any other certificate issued on completion of a course which is a minimum of one day's duration, recognised by the Health and Safety Executive and includes the treatment of hypothermia, cold shock and drowning.

Powerboats

For those with powerboat experience, or with a wish to teach it for a living, the following should provide some guidance as to which course you'd be best suited. This section is for all instructors teaching, or wanting to teach, the RYA Powerboat Scheme. This scheme can be taught in a variety of small open powerboats such as RIBs, dories and sportsboats and is aimed at a variety of users from casual leisure boaters to professional small boat skippers.

Powerboat Instructor

The Powerboat Instructor is a competent, experienced powerboater who has been trained to teach powerboating up to Level 2 under the supervision of the Principal or Chief Instructor of a recognised centre.

Eligibility

- Over 16.
- A least five seasons' experience of powerboating, preferably in a range of boat types and sizes. For those who use powerboats as an integral part of their normal full-time occupation, this period is reduced to one season.
- RYA's Level 2 Powerboat certificate.
- A valid first aid certificate.

Certificate validity Instructor certificates are valid for five years from the date of issue, provided a valid first aid certificate is maintained.

Advanced Powerboat Instructor

Existing Powerboat Instructors wishing to teach the advanced course must be at least 17 years old and hold that level of certificate.

Safety boat instructor training

There is no specific instructor endorsement course for teaching the safety boat course. If you are already a qualified powerboat instructor and hold the safety boat certificate yourself, you may run safety boat courses.

However, please be aware that the training centre at which you are working must hold specific recognition for running that type of course.

Personal Watercraft Instructor

Personal watercraft (PW) instructors are experienced watercraft drivers (such as Jet Skis) who have been trained and assessed to run the RYA's Personal Watercraft Proficiency Course.

PW instructors can now also run the RYA's new Introduction to PW Safety course, which is for guests on superyacht charter holidays.

Eligibility

- Minimum age 16 years.
- RYA personal watercraft proficiency certificate.
- At least two years experience of driving personal watercraft.
- Valid first aid certificate.

Inland Waterways Instructor (IW)

Inland waterways instructors need a great deal of experience and knowledge on the inland waters of the UK, preferably on a variety of craft.

Eligibility

- Inland Waterways Helmsman's Certificate.
- A valid First Aid certificate.
- Marine Radio Operators Short Range Certificate or VHF Operators Certificate.
- Maximum age limit of 65 years.

Shorebased instructors

The Shorebased Instructor course is for anyone wanting to teach the RYA's shorebased navigation and seamanship courses – Basic Navigation and Safety, Day Skipper, Coastal Skipper/Yachtmaster Offshore and Yachtmaster Ocean.

To teach the basic navigation and safety course

Eligibility

- RYA Practical Instructor certificate.
- At least an RYA Day Skipper shorebased course certificate with knowledge well in excess of the Day Skipper shorebased certificate.
- **NB** *RYA Yachtmaster Instructors, Powerboat Trainers and existing Shorebased Instructors can teach this course without further training.*

Qualified navigation instructors are always in demand. Photo – RYA.

To teach the Basic Navigation and Day Skipper Courses

Eligibility

- Advanced Powerboat Instructor certificate.
- Completed the Coastal Skipper/Yachtmaster Offshore shorebased certificate in the last five years, and knowledge should be well in excess of the Coastal Skipper/Yachtmaster Offshore shorebased certificate.

To teach all shorebased courses up to Coastal Skipper/Yachtmaster Offshore

Eligibility

- RYA/MCA Yachtmaster Offshore Certificate of Competence.

- Completed the Coastal Skipper/Yachtmaster Offshore shorebased course in the last five years, and knowledge should be well in excess of that level.

To teach the Yachtmaster Ocean course

Eligibility
- RYA Yachtmaster Instructor or Shorebased Instructor.
- RYA Yachtmaster Ocean Certificate of Competence.

SRC assessors
The SRC (Short Range Certificate) assessor course is for anyone wanting to teach the RYA's marine radio short range certificate course.

Eligibility
- VHF short range certificate.
- RYA instructor in another discipline such as shorebased, cruising, powerboat or dinghy.

Sea survival instructors
The sea survival course is one of the RYA's specialist one-day courses. In order to teach it you must qualify as an RYA sea survival instructor.

Eligibility
- RYA Yachtmaster Instructor or Advanced Powerboat Instructor.
- Sea Survival course certificate.

Diesel instructor
The diesel engine maintenance course is one of the RYA's specialist one-day courses. In order to teach it you must qualify as an RYA diesel instructor, even if you are a qualified marine diesel engineer.

Eligibility
- Good knowledge of the operation and maintenance of marine diesel engines.
- Direct and indirect marine cooling systems and salt water filtration experience.

Radar Instructor

Eligibility
- Experienced in the use of small marine radar and knowledge should be well in excess of the RYA's radar course.

First Aid Instructor

Eligibility
- HSE First Aid at Work certificate, or an equivalent. Doctors, Nurses (UKCC parts 1, 2, 7 or 12) with recent appropriate acute experience and paramedics are exempt from the need

for a first aid certificate, but must be aware of current first aid practices as detailed in the Red Cross/St Johns/St Andrews First Aid Manual.
- VHF or SRC certificate and are normally expected to be an RYA instructor in another field.
- RYA Sea Survival course (highly recommended).

Where to train

There are over 2,300 RYA recognised training establishments worldwide, as well as nationally recognised training schemes in individual countries. The UK-based Royal Yachting Association (RYA), which enforces high standards of marine safety, and the American-based International Yacht Training (IYT), are both accredited by the MCA to run internationally-recognised exams (RYA Yachtmaster and the IYT equivalent – Master of Yachts).

Many of these schools offer fast-track style intensive training for those who want to speed up the qualification process, but the best advice is to contact the RYA who will supply you with a list of centres that specialise in the sort of courses you are looking for.

The level of qualifications you attain will depend on what level you'll be able to teach up to, but inevitably you'll be dealing with novices to start with. Although it might not seem like it at the time, this will be an important period of your teaching career and you'll probably learn more about how to conduct yourself, and how to get the best from your clients, in those first few weeks of training.

One of the best ways of gaining experience in teaching once you have qualified is through one of the many sailing holiday centres in the UK and abroad. You may even find that some companies will, depending on your experience and personality, give you a job as an assistant instructor without any qualifications at all.

Beach holiday teaching

Most beach-based sailing holiday companies such as Sunsail, Neilson, Rockley and Minorca Sailing are always looking for staff for teaching dinghy sailing and windsurfing abroad.

As a guide, a base such as Minorca Sailing will employ around 50 teaching staff during the peak of the season, and although around 50 per cent of these are students, with many on gap years, there is a good balance of ages. Most early career instructors will stay in one position for about four years before moving on and many will see working at these beach holiday centres as a vehicle to gain experience in order to become centre managers when they return to the UK.

These sorts of jobs are, in most cases, extremely low paid with just enough money to buy a few beers at the end of the week. They are also incredibly demanding as far as work load is concerned with just one day off a week. However, if you are looking for somewhere that offers plenty of

Teaching at places like Minorca Sailing provides plenty of opportunities to sail some of the most well-equipped, up-to-date dinghies. Photo – Minorca Sailing.

opportunity to spend time on the water, and provide a good platform in which to base your new teaching career, then a beach sailing holiday centre could be worth thinking about for one season, at least. In a place like Minorca Sailing which specialises in dinghy and windsurfing tuition, you'll also find all the equipment; the windsurfers, rigs and sails are replaced and upgraded on an annual basis which means you, as an instructor, will get to use top-of-the-range kit throughout the season.

It's worth remembering also that as well as Dinghy Instructors, Senior Dinghy Instructors, Windsurfing Instructors, and Senior Windsurfing Instructors who are employed to cover youth and adult sailing, there is a lot of demand for children's instructors, not to mention nannies, and company representatives, so there really is something for everyone.

One of the advantages of teaching in the marine industry is the fact that the RYA schemes are well constructed and progressive, which means there's plenty of scope to allow you to climb the ladder by improving your own qualifications as you go.

Ian Aldridge – Operations Manager at Minorca Sailing – is one of many who have used his time working in the teaching industry as a means of progressing up the teaching ladder. He obtained his initial instructor qualification while working as an assistant instructor, and then went on to gain his Senior Instructor qualification. He is also one of the company's permanent staff, which means when he is not teaching and running the base in Menorca during the summer, he is in the UK at head office planning for the following season.

> 'It's a full on job. I also have to work at major boat shows because this is one of our busiest times for bookings and recruitment.

Teaching theory on the beach is a vital part of learning to sail. Photo – Minorca Sailing.

I always knew I wanted to teach sailing but had to work out the best way of getting my qualifications. I think if you have the drive and passion there is a lot you can do. And certainly using your working time effectively by improving your qualifications as you go, is a really good way to achieve what you want.'

Leaving your previous career behind and heading to the sun to teach sailing for a season may sound like a dream come true, but make sure you are prepared for the change because once you sign up for a job, you can't just keep popping back home to sort out problems. You'll be away for at least seven months so you need to work on the basis you won't have much contact with home and make sure everything, including your house, mortgage, utility bills, car, and anything else you are responsible for, is taken care of.

It's also worth bearing in mind that because you have made the transition from another career, you will probably be older than many of the students you'll be working with on the beach. Because the students you work with will look at you very differently to their peers, you have to make sure your skills levels are high. It's also worth being aware that you will probably be living in communal accommodation, which means sharing living space with those a lot younger than yourself. While this is something most people can cope with for a short period of time, don't forget that you will be working and living together for over six months, which can be fairly challenging.

Other beach jobs

Nanny

Most dinghy and windsurfing holiday centres employ nannies to look after babies and children while their parents enjoy as much time on the water as possible learning new skills.

Beach sailing holiday centres such as Minorca Sailing offer an exceptional service with their qualified team of British nannies who look after and entertain youngsters from four months to four years, seven days a week.

The aim at places like Minorca Sailing, is to maintain a ratio of one nanny to every two babies, and one nanny to every three toddlers which means at the height of the holiday summer season, the company will employ up to five nannies. You may even find that it is possible to combine nanny duties with being a beach sailing instructor if you have the right qualifications. Having transferable skills like this is always seen as an advantage to employers when they are in the process of recruiting new staff.

To look after babies however, you need experienced nannies, and although there is no legal requirement for qualifications to be a nanny, most employers will insist on some form of certification such as Level 3 Diploma in Child Care and Education (CACHE), or Level 3 BTEC National Diploma in Early Years (EDEXCEL), to ensure the nannies are capable of working in an unsupervised environment.

Diving, kitesurfing, canoeing and waterskiing

Most sailing holiday, and outdoor and watersports centres (often run by County Councils) offer other activities in addition to sailing and windsurfing, including diving, kitesurfing, canoeing, sea kayaking, wakeboarding and waterskiing which means qualified specialist staff are always required.

There are many outdoor education courses where you can obtain NGB (National Governing Body) qualifications in canoe coaching, mountain bike leading, climbing wall award, safety and rescue, but it might be worth contacting the organising bodies such as the International Kiteboarding Organisation (ikorg.com), the British sub Aqua Club (bsac.com), the British Canoe Union (bcu.org.uk), and the British Water Ski (britishwaterski.org.uk) who will be able to advise you on recommended training centres should you wish to specialise.

Yacht instruction

Anyone wanting to teach within an RYA recognised practical school on yachts must hold an RYA/MCA Yachtmaster (commercially endorsed) certificate. Yachtmasters who wish to teach to RYA Competent Crew, Helmsman and Day Skipper standards must hold a RYA Cruising Instructors qualification.

This means that if your dream is to teach sailing aboard yachts, the first thing you'll need to do is get qualified. (see Chapter 1 for notes and advice on qualifying).

Anyone wishing to teach at an higher level than RYA Competent Crew, Helmsman and Day Skipper standards must hold an RYA Yachtmaster Instructor qualification.

Qualified sailing instructors are fairly sought after so there's generally a good choice of job opportunities available. Working for well-known sailing holiday/charter companies in the UK and abroad is a good option but don't forget there are many other RYA recognised companies offering an equally good selection of jobs.

Battling against the tidal stream with a yacht full of Competent Crew/Day Skipper students on a cold and windy, rainy day on The Solent may not sound as appealing as island hopping in the blazing sun and clear blue water of the Mediterranean teaching holidaymakers, but knowing you've delivered a good day's tuition and concluded the day with a group of satisfied customers, is equally rewarding.

If you want to steer away from the holiday angle and go down the tuition/training route, sailing schools are always on the look out for good, reliable instructors especially at the height of the summer season. As long as you have the right qualifications, the company (however small) is up to RYA standards, and you are happy with the salary and the conditions they are

A yacht instructor at Ondeck explains the finer details of tuning. Photo – Ondeck/pwpictures.com.

offering, then there's not an awful lot more to worry about. It is advisable however, to do a bit of research by either speaking to other instructors, or training centres to get an idea of the company's background before you accept the job.

Owen Charles, who was in the entertainment business, quit his dancing career and is now a Yachtmaster at Plas Menai National Watersports Centre in Wales. Before he had decided what to do for a career change Charles had never stepped foot on a yacht before. He was a total beginner and didn't really know what to be about as far as a new career was concerned. He initially thought about becoming a school teacher but after a couple of sailing sessions on the South Coast of England which he really enjoyed, the 'penny dropped' and decided to pursue a sailing instructor career. 'I basically went to Plas Menai and did an 18-week zero to hero RYA Yachtmaster course. I then progressed up the ladder and I am now an RYA Yachtmaster Instructor and work on a nine-month seasonal contract at Plas Menai covering courses from Competent Crew up to Yachtmaster preparation.'

Although Charles says he has no doubt that leaving his dancing career to take up a career teaching sailing was a fantastic change, he does stress that the grass is not always greener on the other side: 'If you are thinking about making a career change into the teaching industry remember it's not all about passing exams, it's what happens after that. You basically have to work your socks off to become established. I'd say it took about two years before I got to that stage and was able to relax and enjoy the industry. You have to have a strong sense of determination and have 120 per cent commitment which means, if you have any doubts whether or not it is the right thing for you, you should take more time to consider.'

Training people with mixed abilities to sail while in charge of a yacht can be extremely stressful so you'll need to have the skill to put your clients at ease and be able to remain calm and unflustered when difficult situations arise. Having exceptional communication skills is also an asset when teaching novice sailors.

On RYA cruising courses you're likely to spend five days on board living in close quarters with the same group, on 24-hour call, so it goes without saying you need to have a certain amount of tolerance too. Charles says that time management is probably one of the most important things to remember: 'It is actually time management of yourself. It is important to make sure that when you are away on a yacht with a group of students for a week for example, you take a break by going it alone. It doesn't matter what it is; it can be a walk to the bow of the yacht for a sit down for half an hour, or reading a magazine in your cabin, but whatever it is you have to take time out. That is one of the most important things to remember.'

Earning a decent living from teaching others to sail yachts depends on which company you work for but for a reputable company such as Plas Menai National Watersports Centre, Charles says there are opportunities to earn a reasonable salary. 'For the sort of job I do, the going rate is about £24,000 pro rata. It is not high end by any means, but if you progressed into a more senior position, maybe head of a cruising section, for example you would probably be on something like £28–30,000 per year.'

Other opportunities

As well as a large market for yacht, dinghy, small keelboat and windsurfing and multihull tuition, there's plenty on offer for those who enjoy powerboats. And if you have a dream to work on the inland waterways of the British Isles, why not investigate the Inland Waterways Instructor course. To become an Inland Waterways Helmsman Instructor, which will allow you to teach on a variety of vessels from 7 m (20 ft) motorboats to 21 m (70 ft) narrow boats at one of the many inland waterway RYA recognised training centres, you will need your Inland Waterway Helmsman Course level (IWHC) plus a first aid and VHF/SRC certificates.

Powerboat teaching qualifications are highly regarded and can provide you with endless job opportunities. There are 228 RYA training centres throughout the world specialising in powerboating only, so well qualified powerboat instructors are really sought after. Building up experience in powerboating with at least five season's worth under your belt, plus your Powerboat Level 2 certificate are required before you can take your RYA Powerboat Instructor course.

Teaching disabled sailors

Because sailing is one of the few sports in which able-bodied sailors and disabled sailors can participate on equal terms, disabled sailing is extremely popular. Through Sailability alone – the RYA's disability scheme – over 20,000 people have been able to experience sailing and sail on a regular basis, and there are over 200 dedicated clubs around the UK that run Sailability programmes.

Many of the clubs that run Sailability courses have hoists, launching ramps and specially adapted changing rooms specifically designed for disabled sailors and rely on volunteers to help run the sessions. There are staff positions available but for that you'll need an RYA Instructor's certificate, then because this sort of training is specialised, you'll need to take part in an RYA Sailability Awareness Course which is designed to help you improve personal communication skills, understand the terminology used to explain disability, learn how to use specialist equipment and adaptations, and most importantly practice sailor moving and handling techniques. This is a highly educational course that anyone can sign up for, and it is free of charge. Contact the RYA for more information.

Andy Ramsey, who now runs Yachting Solutions yacht chandlery in Burnham-on-Crouch, originally quit his vehicle mechanic career to become a sailing instructor. As someone who had little sailing experience other than sailing with the Scouts, Ramsey signed up for a three-month fast track Dinghy and Windsurfing Instructor's course at the UKSA on the Isle of Wight. 'It was one of the best things I'd ever done. I had the money in the bank and I wanted some adventure and at 24 years old, I was still relatively young. Actually I loved the course so much I stayed on and did a management course over the winter specialising in business, which has been very useful for me over the last few years.'

One of the best jobs he ever had however, topping all sun-soaked beach holiday-style jobs, was back in the UK teaching sailing in London at the Royal Victoria Docks. Although he confesses to it being probably one of the worst work locations due mainly to the erratic winds created by the high rise offices, he said the actual work, teaching disadvantaged school children and disabled people to sail, was one of the most rewarding he has ever had.

> 'The school was run under the borough of Newham so there were secondary school children from all sorts of backgrounds including those with not much discipline.
>
> Some of them just didn't want to learn. I had one young lad who was a cheeky little monkey to say the least. One day I sat down with him and had a casual chat and discovered that despite his lively exterior, he had a bit of an aim because he said wanted to go to college and study. The problem he had was lack of support at home, which wasn't surprising given the fact his dad, brother and uncle were always in jail and I think his granddad was too.
>
> The amazing thing was he was always sensible on the water so it just goes to show that given the opportunities youngsters like this can benefit enormously.'

Teaching disadvantaged children to sail is one thing but teaching disabled people – children and adults – is even more rewarding. As far as looking for job satisfaction in a new career is concerned, this is at the top of the list according to Ramsey. 'I would say working with disabled sailors is by far the most rewarding job in the marine industry. It is hard, hard work because you have to think on your feet a lot more and you need to have the right sort of calm personality.

'I think most of the groups I used to teach spent longer putting on their wetsuits than they did sailing, but do you know what? It didn't matter. If I had to recommend a job to anyone, that would be it. Job satisfaction is 100 percent.'

Another popular area of work involving disabled sailors is aboard Sail Training ships (see separate section on page 88).

Teaching shorebased courses

If you are a qualified shorebased instructor and want to specialise in that area there are plenty of RYA training establishments worldwide always on the look out for professionals to work

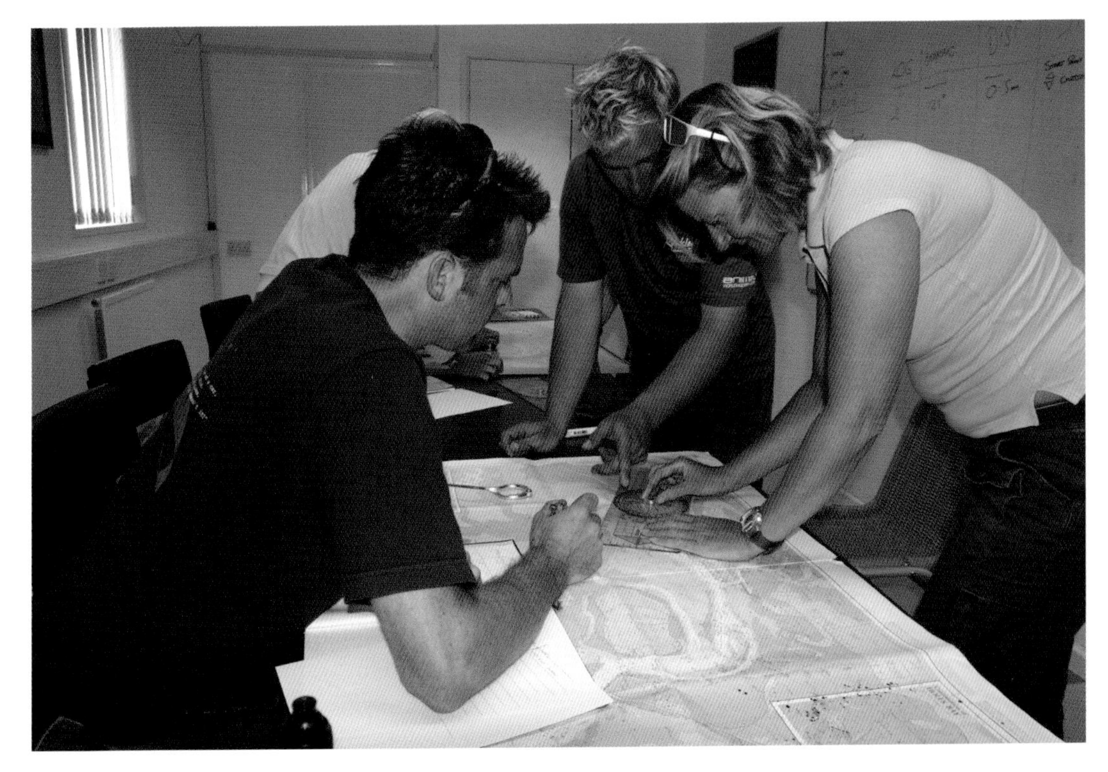

Shorebased theory courses help students learn navigational skills. Photo – RYA.

on a part time or full time basis. As you will find out when you are going through your own qualification process, all courses afloat are complemented by the RYA's shorebased courses, which offer tuition in navigation, sea survival, and other specialist subjects.

Alternatively you might consider going it alone and setting up your own teaching centre, which is incredibly simple to do and costs around £100 to be RYA recognised. The only equipment you'll need is a couple of laptops, a board, and the all-important kettle!

According to Simon Jinks, the RYA don't stipulate where you run it, although he says running courses in your front room is probably not going to work. 'If you are marketing the courses and want to charge £300 for example, you really can't run it from home with the dog running around warming your clients' feet, or have the sound of the TV in the other room in the background, or both. It's just not right.'

Also remember that working from home raises all sorts of issues. For a start you will need public liability insurance just in case, for example, one of your clients tripped up on the doormat and broke their leg.

With this in mind, the best way to go about it is to rent a presentation room in a local hotel, yacht club, or even a meeting room in an office complex, or wherever is available and convenient. This will not only ensure the courses are run in the most professional environment but will also ensure you keep your work separate from home life.

Sail Training

Sail training is not to be confused with training to sail but a term used to define an opportunity for people of all ages and abilities including youth, those with disabilities, and members of the older generation, to experience crewing as a trainee aboard sail training vessels.

Although square-rigged tall ships (those fitted with square-shaped looking sails) are a popular choice of sail training vessels, particularly in countries where they are used for military training, any yacht regardless of size, can be used for sail training.

So what is sail training, who runs it, and what sort of job opportunities are available? Sail training is open to people of all ages and abilities and is an extremely popular way of teaching the principles of responsibility, resourcefulness, loyalty, and team endeavour. Above all, it is the perfect platform in which to demonstrate the art of seamanship.

Working aboard Sail Training vessels is one of the best ways of seeing the world. Here the Indonesian ship *Dewaruci*, and *Shabab Oman*, arrive in Varna, Bulgaria for the STI Historical Seas Regatta. Photo – Sue Pelling.

The Association of Sail Training Organisations (ASTO), the national sail training organisation in the UK, is a member of Sail Training International (STI) the international body which oversees sail training throughout the world. ASTO is a charitable organisation set up to promote opportunities for sea training under sail or power in the UK and, through the provision of bursaries, offers assistance for those who need help with funding.

There are over 30 member organisations of ASTO in the UK including the Jubilee Sailing Trust, Cirdan Sailing Trust, and Tall Ships Youth Trust many of whom employ full-time staff in addition to volunteers. There was a time when most of the crew on sail training vessels worked voluntarily but because of legislation and the need to have professional qualifications there are more and more jobs being created. At Cirdan Sailing Trust for example – whose aim it is to give disadvantaged young people an opportunity for self-development through the experience of living and working on large sailing boats – all skippers, mates, and bosuns are employed full-time during the working season.

On some of the larger sail training ships such as the British-registered vessel *Royalist* there are six full-time staff including the Captain, mate, an engineer, cook, bosun in charge of the rig, a coxwain in charge of everything below decks.

According to Lucy Gross – ASTO Manager – most people coming into the Sail Training world will probably have had previous experience as a volunteer or trainee in the past. 'The reason I now work in the sail training industry is down to the fact that when I was 16 I went on a sail training ship. It was such an amazing experience and I became hooked on the idea that I wanted to work with tall ships one day. For me there were two attractions and these are the key qualities to think about if you are considering working in the industry: the idea of working with sailing, and working with children.'

To work in sail training therefore you will need qualifications and although these will vary depending on the size of yacht you intend to work aboard (above or below 24 m [72 ft]) they follow the same principles as other RYA/MCA exams. If your aim is to one day become a captain

A mate aboard the Danish sail training vessel *Loa* carries out vital rope work. Photo – Sue Pelling.

of a large (above 60 m [180 ft]) tall ship then it is imperative you obtain some experience in the art of square rig sailing by either going onboard a ship as a volunteer, or by signing up for a course at somewhere like the Square Sail Shipyard in Cornwall where it is possible to get your Square Sail certificate in Square Rig Seamanship.

It is also worth investigating the ASTO Skippership Scheme, which is a structured programme that draws together the skills required to work as a sea-going Sail Trainer in the modern Sail Training industry.

Gross says that spending time aboard a tall ship to see if you take to it is highly recommended: 'As obvious as it might sound, it is really important to find out before you invest too much time or money in the idea. When you go onboard as a volunteer there is always feedback from the organisation you go with. It is quite thorough because they sit down with you and give recommendations about how you should go forward, which means it is a really good way of finding out if you are suitable to pursue the career further.'

The challenge and adventure of sailing tall ships on the open sea is one of the best ways to promote integration of people of all physical abilities. According to the Jubilee Sailing Trust (JST) – a member of ASTO – there are over 10.8 million people with a disability in the UK, 6.9 million of whom are of working age – which equates to just over 18 per cent, almost one fifth, of the UK's entire working age population. With this in mind it is good to see that organisations such as the JST are raising the awareness and understanding of how sailing can provide huge benefits to those with disabilities by using two specially adapted ships – *Tenacious* and *Lord Nelson*. Both JST ships are sailed by full-time professional sailors and 40 voyage crew of mixed physical ability and often referred to as trainees. There are therefore plenty of job opportunities on ships like these so it's always worth investigating. The sort of jobs likely to come up on sail training ships include:

- Captain (or Master)
- Mate (or 1st Mate, 1st Officer)
- 2nd Mate (or 2nd Officer)
- Bosun (or 3rd Mate / Officer)
- Chief Engineer
- 2nd Engineer
- Medical Purser
- Cook.

Simon Catterson joined the marine industry after ten years in the Navy. He is now the Captain of *Tenacious* one of the largest tall ships in the world working for the Jubilee Sailing Trust. He had to work his way up the ladder from Second Mate, Mate and Relief Master before taking on the full-time position as Captain, but says it is one of the most rewarding jobs you can ever hope to have: 'The great thing about it is the huge range of people we have to deal with. It's not only the abilities, but also the different generations and the different backgrounds. We're dealing with people aged from 16 up to 99, but there is no upper age limit. We have lots of guys in their 70s and 80s who sail with us, even in their 90s. It's all in a day's work and it's incredibly rewarding.'

With a wife and young son at home, going away for long stints is fairly tough but Catterson believes it works well. 'I'm away eight months out of 12 but it's usually in four to six week periods so it's manageable. My son has never yet said 'who's that strange man!'

One of the most negative aspects of the job, as in a lot of jobs within the marine industry, is the pay. 'In this sort of job you are likely to earn probably less than half you'd expect in the commercial world and not even in the same universe as you'd get in private yachts. I live a comfortable life however, and really enjoy my job. I'd say 94 per cent of the time I have one of the best jobs in the world. Five per cent of the time it's okay, and one per cent of the time I think 'what the hell am I doing here?' You really can't do much better than that.'

Finding jobs in sail training

One of the best ways of finding a job in the sail training industry is by visiting the ASTO website – asto.org.uk. There is usually always an assortment of sail training type jobs available particularly in the off season [winter]. Most ships start their season in March and will need to have staff vacancies filled by then. The Sail Training International website is also a good resource. It is unlikely you'll find these sorts of specialist jobs in sailing magazines but crew agency websites such as crewseekers are also worth a look.

Setting up your own sailing school

UK based

There are various ways to go about setting up your own sailing school, either on your own where you base your company around the use of clients' dinghies or yachts for teaching purposes, or using your own vessel. The other way, which will require more investment, is setting up a shore-based company with facilities, and yachts/dinghies (that you either own or charter) for teaching.

The first route requires relatively little investment as far as equipment and facilities are concerned and you might be surprised at how easy the process is because a sailing school that uses the client's own dinghy or yacht for training purposes has no legal responsibilities as it is down to the client to ensure the vessel is in safe, working order.

You will, however, need to be qualified which will inevitably be not only your biggest investment as far as cost is concerned but also the time for the qualification process. If you are fortunate enough to already have sailing qualifications and you have the ability to teach, then the only other things to consider is purchasing a RIB (Rigid Inflatable Boat) for on the water training purposes and some good quality warm, waterproof sailing clothing and footwear.

Should you decide to run a bigger sailing school by investing in yachts/dinghies, equipment and onshore facilities, you should be aware of the legislation regarding coding of yachts used for commercial purposes (see MCA coding of yachts for commercial use on page 23). Simon Jinks – who formerly ran the RYA Yachtmaster programme for sail and motor vessels, and the RYA navigation and safety courses, and who now runs the Sea Regs consultancy, says there are a few basic things to remember when setting up alone. 'Any boats you purchase for the school need to come up to national standard. Basically, if it is part of the small boat scheme such as dinghy, windsurfing and powerboating and it's just doing RYA stuff, you can work under the RYA umbrella, but if it is a cruising yacht or motorboat, or a powerboat going further offshore, then it needs to be MCA coded. The RYA have worked exemptions with the MCA for most of the small boats, so as long as the boat comes up to the standards in the guidelines layed down by the RYA, and as they are annually inspected, the MCA are pretty happy.'

If you want to run an RYA school running RYA courses you'll have to invest in equipment such as boats, and provide facilities up to relevant standards. As an owner of an RYA Recognised School, you don't necessarily have to be a qualified RYA instructor to run it, but the staff you employ must be qualified to the right level. For example the centre must employ a Chief Instructor who holds an RYA Yachtmaster Certificate with a current Yachtmaster Instructor's endorsement (Power and/or Sail).

One of the most important aspects of running any sailing school however, is the paperwork involved such as the Safety Management System, which supports clients from the booking process all the way through until they have completed their course.

Knowing exactly what is required when setting up a sailing school therefore, can be fairly daunting so it's worth tracking down someone who has gone through a similar process and who would be willing to advise. Ideally, you need to speak to someone who specialises in these sorts of issues such as SeaRegs. This company offers unbiased technical advice and support to commercial organisations, authorities and individuals and covers all aspects of requirements for setting up your own sailing school/charter company including MCA codes of practice, and Safety Management Systems. Investing in this sort of advice (approximately £250 per day) could save you not only a lot of time, but also a lot of worry. It's a bit like having an accountant to take away the burden of something you know little about, leaving you more time to concentrate on setting up your new business.

Other important issues to remember when setting up an RYA sailing school that has boats and facilities for commercial use, are the initial and annual inspection by the RYA. Because of its RYA status, the school will need to maintain the RYA's high standards. The cost for this varies depending on whether the school is in the UK or abroad. Generally speaking the initial Training Centre Recognition set-up fees range from £310–£900, while the annual inspection fees are from £260–£600.

The latest guidance, rules and regulations regarding setting up an RYA recognised training centre are available from the RYA. The particular documents you need to read, which are updated on an annual basis, include:

- Guidance Notes For Sail and Motor Cruising
- Training Centres Inspection form (IR1)
- Training Vessel Checklist.

Sailing instructor Melvyn Cooper explains dinghy sailing skills during a one-to-one session. Photo – Melvyn Cooper.

The RYA say that compliance with these documents, forms the basis for initial and continuing RYA recognition.

Melvyn Cooper who was the UK Sales Manager for a country clothing and footwear company chose to take voluntary redundancy in 2009. After a lot of research and having such a passion for the sport of sailing, he decided to set up his own dinghy sailing school, based on Chichester Harbour and specialising in one-to-one style tuition in clients' own boats.

Cooper commenting on his career change said: 'The redundancy couldn't have come at a better time in some ways because it allowed me to take the summer off and rethink my career. I spent most of the time on the beach helping out at my club (Hayling Island Sailing Club) and it all went from there really.'

Going about it the correct way, Cooper qualified as an RYA Dinghy Instructor with advanced module and RYA Race coach Level 2, and he says that the plan is to progress and gain his RYA Senior Instructor certificate. According to Cooper, once the research was done, setting up was fairly straight forward. 'The plan of action was to provide a quality coaching service and build up a customer base over three years. I researched competition and networked with other instructors and coaches and found a spot in the market.'

Because Cooper generally works on a one-to-one basis aboard the clients' own boats, he is in the fortunate position of not having sailing school facilities. 'I coach at various sailing clubs in Chichester Harbour and other clubs in the south of England, and because I coach sailors by sailing with them in their own boat, or use the sailing club RIB, my initial outlay has been minimal. My aim however, is to buy my own RIB eventually because this will provide more independence.'

One of the most difficult areas Cooper experienced when setting up was the Criminal Records Bureau (CRB) check which can be carried out by contacting www.crb.homeoffice.gov.uk. 'I think the problems arise because it is not aimed at the individual running their own business. However, my advice is to persist. The easiest way I found was to obtain clearance through the help of an organisation.'

Once you've set up and registered your business, you're priority is marketing. A website for your new business is an essential component so make sure you secure a website domain name as soon as you can, and if necessary appoint a specialist to build you an effective website. Ensure the site is clear, concise with your own distinct identity and, most importantly, make sure it is simple to navigate. You need to make it easy for prospective clients to find what they are looking for. And, as obvious as it may sound, don't forget to ensure your company contact details including telephone number, are included on the Home page.

Cooper said that although word of mouth is important, particularly in the early stages of setting up, having your own website is where most business will come from. 'Also, once you have built a database of names, e-mail shots are a good way of promoting your business.'

As most who are self-employed find, particularly those working as a sole trader, the workload is phenomenal, particularly in the first year or two while you are setting up and establishing your business. However, as most will tell you, the freedom of running your own business, being your own boss, and the ultimate rewards, far outweigh the hard work. Cooper added: 'It's true, it's full on but being able to teach people my passion of sailing rather than sitting in an office, is incredibly rewarding. Because it is a seasonal job with summer full on, it is important to make sure I have some time off during the winter and 'shoulder' parts of the season. Having said that, this is still a busy time for me as I use it to prepare for the new season.'

Making a profit in the first year of any business is challenging and although Cooper said the first year of trading did not provide a financial living, in balance he has a different way of life. 'It's no different to any other business but I am confident that in the future it will provide me with a living and a very fulfilling way of life.'

Setting up a sailing school overseas

Embarking on setting up an RYA recognised sailing school in the UK is – relatively speaking – fairly straightforward once you get the paperwork sorted and have a firm understanding of safety and the laws. Setting up a sailing base abroad however, will be a lot more challenging so you need to follow advice from either those who've carried out a similar project in the past, or by recruiting a specialist consultant to provide guidance and make sure you don't forget any important issues.

As a guide here are some examples of some of the extra conditions you'll need to think about for setting up an RYA sailing centre abroad:

- The sailing centre is required to have a permanent address abroad.
- The language of instruction should be English, and translation is not permitted.
- All students will be provided with course feedback reports as and when required by the RYA.
- The sailing centre needs to pay an overseas recognition fee, and will also be liable to pay the inspector's expenses from his/her departure airport, including flights, accommodation and subsistence.
- The sailing centre needs to have Third Party liability insurance of £2,000,000 and be adequately insured to fulfil its legal responsibilities.

A full list of conditions can be found in the RYA's Guidance Notes for Sail and Motor Crusing Training Centres.

Alan Hilman's sailing centre – Pro-Vela – specialises in high performance dinghy holidays and training. Photo – pro-vela.com.

British sailor Alan Hillman who's been passionate about sailing from a young age, always knew he wanted to run his own sailing school one day.

Because of this his education was very much sports based which meant when he did decide to take the plunge and set up a sailing school abroad, he already had his feet well and truly on the teaching sailing career ladder. 'I was lucky enough to do a sports based degree where I worked as an instructor during the holidays. I later completed a PGCE, so being a qualified teacher helped my CV stand out. The sailing industry is also a pretty small world so if you get yourself a good reputation, it is really easy to get on . . . or not . . . if you do not cut the mustard!'

Convinced he was cut out for teaching, Hillman added to his BSc (Hons) sports science, and PGCE with a host of useful RYA coaching certificates in dinghy, keelboats, powerboats, and PWCs (Jet Skis) but he says he still values his Yachtmaster Offshore qualification the most. He became the RYA Windsurfing Manager, and then, armed with plenty of qualifications Hillman set up a sailing school in Mar Menor, Spain with a British business partner and former RYA 470 Olympic coach Rob Andrews. Since then, Hillman has taken over the centre completely and it now runs under the name Pro-Vela which specialises in high performance dinghy holidays/training.

According to Hillman, the initial plan was to base the centre somewhere in Europe:

> 'In our opinion, the only way to make a small fortune in sailing is to start with a large one, so with a lot of history and knowledge in the sport behind us, and a lot of good contacts, we started looking for a location.
>
> It had to be near an airport, so we started drawing 100 km circles around airports. We had a bit of a Eureka moment when we circled Alicante. Both Rob and I had been to the Mar Menor before in a coaching or competitor capacity and both immediately knew that was the place we wanted to locate our sailing centre. We approached the Spanish Tourist Board in London and thankfully they loved our business plan and flew us out and helped find a location. I believe we were really lucky on that one!'

Interestingly, Hillman says that setting up a sailing school/holiday centre in Spain is not as difficult as you first imagine but there is a lot of bureaucracy and strange laws that can be confusing. 'Basically, the laws are a nightmare and open to interpretation, so you must do your homework and ideally get good, local help. There is no body like the RYA in Spain, so you work through the local bodies such as the town hall, coastal authorities and harbour master, and each location is different. You'll also find there is no co-ordination between the coast guard and the town halls so it can be frustrating navigating your way to get a licence. The funniest thing is that once you have applied for a licence you may not actually get it until the end of the season!'

All in all Hillman says he has a fantastic lifestyle but it takes a while to understand the culture differences in business. 'I must say, it is hard not to like the laid back lifestyle until, that is, you have to work in it. For a north European like me, it was a bit of a culture shock. As far as profitability is concerned well, it pays the bills but it certainly won't send your kids to private school.'

As with most hobby-led jobs, it's worth remembering there is a risk that you might not be able to enjoy the sport you are so passionate about in the same way, once it's incorporated within your new career. If you set up your own business, you'll probably find that you sail less often than you used to. Hillman says this is definitely one of the negative aspects to it: 'Sailing is the part I love and enjoy but having a sailing business means spending more time running the business than actually sailing.'

If you do have an ambition to set up business on your own either abroad or in the UK it pays to remember a few basic pieces of advice: research, a good business plan, and running a good marketing campaign. Hillman, confirming what others who run businesses in the marine industry reveal, says: 'Marketing is the most expensive commodity and getting the word out is not easy or cheap, but it has to be done, and it has to be done correctly.'

How to find teaching jobs

Once you have decided on the route you want to take, which will undoubtedly mean getting yourself qualified, you can start investigating the jobs on the market. Teaching jobs are specialised so you need to look in the right area. There are 2,500 RYA sailing schools/teaching establishments including shorebased centres around the globe making contact with sailing schools in the vicinity is worthwhile, and familiarising yourself with some of the well known sailing schools/holiday company websites will also give you an indication of what's available. You may find there's a recruitment page where you have to provide details of the sort of job you are looking for. This is a great idea and most companies will be aware of the implications of data protection but just be careful not to provide too much personal information which may be published on a website.

One of the best ways of finding a job is through the RYA's Wavelength publication which goes out to all RYA qualified instructors, coaches, trainers and examiners. You'll find a lot of UK based RYA recognised training establishments advertise for teaching staff in there. You'll also be able to obtain a lot of career advice from the training centre where you take your exams. Centres like the UKSA on the Isle of Wight, which specialise in career training are always keen to help their students secure a job once they have seen them through the qualification process.

Jim Prendergast – Chief Instructor at Ondeck – says that as a freelancer looking for a job you have to be prepared to apply yourself, and be extremely professional. 'When I am looking to employ freelance instructors I need them to be qualified for the position and most importantly I need them to be easy to employ. In our company we sign up freelance instructors sometimes on a day-to-day basis which means if they are on our books, they need to be flexible. Ideally they should provide a list of available dates, and be reliable.'

Chapter 5
Professional racing

If you enjoy sailing, have a competitive spirit, and are the sort of person who has to achieve certain goals in life, you may think the professional racing circuit could be the place for you. Imagine all those weekends and holidays you spend enjoying sailing, competing at your local club, taking part in championships in the UK and abroad, or racing at high profile events such as the Rolex Fastnet Race, Round the Island Race, or even Cowes Week. How spectacular would it be therefore, to be able to extend your passion for sailing into a career, and get paid for it? Never again would you have to endure that Monday morning commute to the office because you'd be out on the water living your dream.

Although the thought of turning your hobby into a career sounds like a sparkling idea, it's worth keeping it in perspective before diving into the deep end of this particular option. In reality, to become a professional racing sailor ideally you need to have a strong sailing background with plenty of experience in all sectors of the sport including dinghy sailing and sailing on yachts. Having a successful racing background is beneficial, although not essential, as many of today's professional ocean racers have proved.

If you do decide you have what it takes to pit yourself against the best sailors in the world however, and want to give racing for a living a go, one of the key things to remember is, unless you are independently wealthy, or fortunate enough to secure a good sponsorship deal to fund the campaign you have in mind, then the chances are, money will be extremely tight and probably non-existent while you build up your reputation to prove you are worthy of being paid to go sailing.

Olympic 470 sailors Stuart Bithell and Christian Birrel demonstrating the fun side of professional sailing. Photo – Julio Graham.

Pete Cumming, a champion Extreme 40 skipper on the professional circuit, who started life off as a dinghy sailing 'jockey' for a chandlery that produced championship winning racing dinghies and sails, said that although he gets to travel the world, sail on some amazing boats with some amazing people, and cannot think of anything he would rather do, finding work on the professional circuit is always challenging.

> 'Owners move on and teams and sponsors change. You are rarely contracted to a team for more than a season, and this is in the best case. You have to be tough and not get scared off by rejection from teams. The work is inconsistent and generally the time between events is spent trying to negotiate the next ride . . . which is tough! Although you do get time at home you will end up spending large chunks of time away from home and you have to be flexible to be able to drop everything last minute should the call come in from a team, and also be prepared for plans to be turned on their head last minute too.'

Mike Golding OBE, one of the world's most talented and respected offshore/round the world sailors, added: 'Without question, the possibilities of making a living from sailing are increasing as the sport develops a wider appeal to sponsors. If you are a good enough sailor and are prepared to get out there at every opportunity, then there's every chance of making it. The sport is still quite cliquey in the UK however, which is bad – a legacy of the past – so you do still need to know the right people to get the opportunities.'

There are various ways of earning a living as a professional racing sailor so you'll need to decide which area of the sport you'd be best suited to. Unlike other sectors of the industry such as teaching, working on a charter yacht, or delivering yachts, professional racing has no real career structure to it which means it's down to you to work out a plan and decide how to go forwards with it. Having RYA qualifications are not essential but highly recommended particularly if you intend to go down the big boat route and want to work on commercial yachts while you are building up experience.

The following are a selection of professional sailor roles you might like to consider:

- **Dinghy sailing jockey** – talented dinghy sailors are employed by sailmakers, spar (mast) makers, or builders for the research and development process of products, and to demonstrate the products' potential through good results on the race course.
- **Olympic sailor** helmsman/crew – highly talented sailor who has a proven successful racing record and been selected as representative in the Olympic Games.
- **Offshore solo sailor –** helmsman who competes alone in races like the Vendée Globe, Velux 5 Oceans Race or Mini Transat.

- **Professional yacht racing crew** – employed to produce winning results on the racecourse, ranging from round-the-world ocean racing, to round the buoys inshore racing:
- **Skipper** – in overall charge of the boat.
- **Tactician** – manages immediate situations and anticipates as much as possible including monitoring direct competition.
- **Helmsman (dinghies and yachts)**– steers the boat.
- **Navigator** – responsible for all aspects of navigation, strategy and weather.
- **Bow** – athletic member of crew in charge of the front end of the boat. In constant communication with the helmsman.
- **Trimmer** – setting the sails for optimum performance.

Deciding in which area to specialise will depend on your previous experience and the sort of challenges you think you are prepared to undertake. Racing on the professional circuit, whether

The Extreme 40 professional racing circuit attracts many of the world's top sailors. Photo – Mark Lloyd/ Lloyd Images.

in dinghy, small keelboat or offshore yachts, it is extremely high profile so you need to be sure you have the ability to face the challenges head on.

Ian Williams is a former World Match Racing Tour champion who became the first Briton to be crowned match racing World Champion in the event's 19-year history. Sponsored by Pindar, he skippers Team GAC Pindar's Extreme 40 in the Extreme Sailing Series, but he originally trained as a lawyer. His initial idea was to combine his legal career with Olympic sailing and it worked out well, but the Soling class in which Williams was racing was dropped as an Olympic class, forcing him to rethink his career. He continued match racing while working as a lawyer but when he started notching up respectable results on the world match racing circuit, he took a six-month sabbatical from his job and in that time won two Grade 1 events, which gave him the confidence to quit his job and take up sailing full time.

According to Williams, one of the biggest frustrations with sailing as a professional sport is its lack of governance and clear direction. The best way to take it on is to identify a role and believe

Tips from the top

Ben Ainslie CBE

Ben Ainslie is Britain's most successful Olympic sailor having won three Olympic gold medals, and a silver. He is also one of the world's most talented America's Cup helmsmen.

Photo – Mark Lloyd/Lloyd Images

Ben's advice to succeed as an Olympic sailor:

- You need 100 per cent commitment, which means you need to have the ability to understand that your life will change dramatically. You'll be away from home, family and friends the majority of the time, and having a social life and building friendships can be difficult.
- Motivation and the will to win are essential. And even when times are tough, you need to have the strength to move on and learn from mistakes.
- Having the ability to listen, learn and understand other points of view, and being professional at all times, are probably some of the most important qualities to have. Also never forget those who helped you on your road to success.

that you can be better at that role than the people currently doing it. Talking about his career path Williams said:

> 'Because I wanted to go to the Olympics I got very good at match racing a Soling. Suddenly, less than three years before the Athens Olympics, the Soling class was dropped as an Olympic class. Later on my goal has been the America's Cup and I have worked hard on the skills, the match racing skills that appeared to be required. Now that skill set has changed dramatically, this time with three years' notice. In hindsight perhaps I should have focused on other areas of the sport, but with what I knew at the time, I am happy with the decisions that I have made.'

Dinghy and small keelboat racing

Olympic sailor

With a risk of sounding pessimistic to the highest degree, the chances of leaving one career to become an Olympic sailor are extremely slim. Olympic class sailing is exceptionally high profile, and those who make a living from it have, in most cases, spent their life working up to that level, which means realistically you need to have started young.

If you feel you have exceptional talent however, and think there is a chance of making it to Olympic level, you need to make contact with the Royal Yachting Association and find out how to get involved with the Olympic scene. You'll then need to prove – with consistent results on the race course – you have what it takes to be considered as part of the Skandia Olympic Squad. It is a long process and, remember there are only a handful of sailors from hundreds of extremely talented sailors who campaign to get in the team, who ever make it to that level.

Most Olympic sailors such as Ben Ainslie (triple Olympic gold medallist in the Laser and Finn classes), Iain Percy (double gold medallist in the Finn and Star classes) have been competing all their lives and have progressed through the RYA Olympic system to reach Olympic standard. Because of their training, on and off the water, they are among some of the fittest athletes in the world. Being an Olympic sailor of that calibre requires total commitment on and off the water, and an understanding that the success of their career is all about consistently producing results of the highest standards.

Dinghy sailing jockey

If you are a talented dinghy sailor and want to earn a living from racing other than going down the Olympic route, there are opportunities to get signed up as what is known as a 'jockey.' This is where specialist companies such as sailmakers, spar (mast) makers, or boat builders employ

Triple Olympic gold medallist Ben Ainslie is 100 per cent dedicated to succeeding on the race course. Photo – Mark Lloyd/Lloyd Images.

sailors to become involved in the research and development process of their products, and to demonstrate the products' potential through good results on the race course.

These sorts of jobs are relatively sought after because not only do they offer an opportunity to go sailing and get paid for it, they give the employee the chance of testing out pioneering ideas. Those fortunate enough to have worked as a jockey will tell you how extremely rewarding it is to be part of the R&D (research and development) team, sail with brand-new kit all the time, and get paid for it. It also provides a great opportunity to learn and build up a reputation on the circuit, which could lead to future career opportunities.

Pete Cumming who is now a champion Extreme 40 skipper on the professional circuit, started life off as a jockey for a chandlery that produced championship winning racing dinghies and sails. Cumming commented: 'With new dinghies to sail, a car, and a list of major national and international regattas to compete at, I thought life doesn't get much better than this. It was

Tips from the top

Pete Cumming

Pete Cumming started his professional sailing career as a dinghy sailing jockey but is now a world champion skipper on the professional Extreme 40 circuit.

Photo – Mark Lloyd/Lloyd Images

Pete's advice on surviving as a professional skipper:

- Don't make rash decisions; let your head rule not your heart.
- Always leave doors open behind you and make sure you deliver to the team.
- Make sure you have a few options of boats to sail and try to get a commitment from the team for the amount of days/events they will be using you. Again this can be fickle as it is easy to be promised the season and then this fades away to nothing, other sailors come into the mix or the budgets are cut. It is surprising how often this is the case.
- Have a practical skill base that you can take to the team.

a great life experience and I certainly wouldn't have got where I am today without that job. I would recommend it to anyone who wants to progress on the pro circuit.'

Small keelboats

Small keelboats have similar sailing characteristics to dinghies but have a fixed keel rather than a lifting centreboard which means they are less likely to capsize. They are usually sailed by two or more crew and are popular day racing boats. There are numerous designs on the market including Etchells, Dragons, Ynglings, Squibs, Solings, Flying 15s, and hundreds of local one-design keelboats such as XODs, Darings, Royal Burnham One-Design and Fowey Troys. Many of these classes are extremely old, yet because of their one-design status (identical designs), still offer some exceptionally close racing. There are also two keelboat classes among the ten-strong Olympic class fleets; the Elliott 6 m (women), and Star (men), and there are many small keelboats around the world that are popular for match racing.

Among the largest and most popular of the small keelboats is the International Dragon, which often sees over 100 boats on the start line of international regattas. This popular one-design which is over 80 years old was also an Olympic class spanning seven Olympic Games between

1948–1972. Over the years the design has developed and is now one of the most sophisticated racing boats in the world, which means it attracts high profile sailors including those from the America's Cup and Olympic sectors who come into the fleet to enjoy close racing. But the fleet is not restricted to professional sailors by any means, in fact the majority of the fleet is made up of club sailors from around the world who enjoy being able to compete and learn from the high calibre fleet.

Martin Payne (aka Stravros) who is a professional sailor specialises in the Dragon fleet, sailing with owners to help improve their performance. Payne's original career was teaching sports and maths at Torquay Boys Grammar School, Devon. This he did for 19 years but following a divorce, he decided to quit and make a fresh start. 'It was a now or never situation and I've never looked back.'

Payne was involved in the class and became successful by starting to win significant events internationally which meant he had a basis on which to expand his idea to combine his teaching experience with sailing. He started building up a list of clients whose performance he was able to help improve on the racecourse. 'I am convinced that all the experience I had as a teacher in

Tips from the top

Mike Golding OBE

Photo – Mark Lloyd/Lloyd Images

Mike Golding, who switched his fire-fighting career to become a professional sailor, is now one of the world's most talented and respected offshore/round the world sailors. Golding has endless sailing achievements under his belt but his greatest ambition is to win the Vendée Globe – an event that has so far eluded him.

Mike's advice on how to succeed on the professional racing circuit:

- Be a team player, which means getting on with others and communicating well are essential.
- Learn as much as you can about business and management skills because as well as sailing you'll need to deal with the business aspects of your campaign.

my former career, gave me the edge over other top sailors who fail to get their points across to customers/clients.'

'I started on around £75 (sterling), per day, plus expenses. And would not only move the Dragons around Europe, but also collect the owners from airports, get them into their nice hotels whilst I rigged the boat, tuned it and basically taught them to sail at a higher level.'

Over the last 13 years Payne has won numerous Dragon Championships and says his daily rate has now increased: 'My daily rate now is 800 Euros, so life is not so bad.'

Combining your skills and having the ability to seek a niche in a market is certainly a good option, but like Payne, you need to be totally dedicated and involved in a class in order to succeed. You also have to be prepared to market yourself. Payne concluded: 'Being at every regatta is vitally important. I meet more clients every regatta, so it is really worthwhile. I also enjoy it, of course.'

Former car mechanic Steve White sets off on the Vendée Globe singlehanded, non-stop round the world race. Photo – Bernard Gergaud/White Ocean Racing.

Round the world racing

Round the world sailors are some of the toughest crews you are ever likely to meet. Sailing 40,000 miles round the globe on pioneering, state-of-the-art carbon fibre racing machines, living off freeze-dried food, little sleep and battling with hostile conditions with temperatures ranging from –5 to +40 degrees Celsius, is the ultimate test of human endeavour.

Going Solo

There can be few people not impressed with the amazing performance of the great sailors who race some of the most complex machines around the world – singlehandedly. Take Dame Ellen MacArthur, who through sheer determination, reached her ultimate goal of successfully completing a 27,000-mile circumnavigation in a 25 m (75 ft) multihull, and breaking the world speed record with a time of 71 days, 14 hours, 18 minutes, 33 seconds in 2005. While there is no doubt that MacArthur, who was 28 years old at the time, possesses exceptional qualities to physically have been able to carry out a feat like this, it was her passion for sailing that ultimately led her to success.

Rather than racing against the clock, alone, as MacArthur did, the more popular way of racing round the world is to take part in one of the organised global races such as the Vendée Globe. This is a non-stop, singlehanded round the world race in 20 m (60 ft) high performance racing machines known as Open 60 s or IMOCA 60 s (International Monohull Open Class Association). The race takes place every four years and starts and finishes in Les Sables d'Olonne, France and the overall winner is the first one to cross the finish line. The 30,000-mile Velux 5 Oceans Race is equally as tough (starting and finishing in La Rochelle, France), but in this race competitors have a chance to recover and make repairs during five stopover ports positioned around the globe and it's a double-handed race.

Although MacArthur did learn to sail from a relatively young age and therefore built up a lot of experience before she embarked on her record-breaking voyage, there are plenty of global sailors out there who started off their careers relatively new to the sailing game, many having come from previous careers.

Mike Golding is a classic example of someone who switched careers and made a big success of his life. Golding was a former fire fighter who became a professional following a second place skippering *Group 4* in the British Steel Challenge in 1992/93 and is now one of the world's most talented and respected offshore/round the world sailors. Golding wasn't totally new to sailing when he did the round the world race on Group 4 because he spent his youth sailing dinghies and windsurfing, but it was the Global Challenge that really highlighted his competitive spirit. His transition into the IMOCA 60 class aboard the fully-sponsored Open 60 *Ecover* however, was where he really made his name. Golding's ambition is to win a race, which has so far eluded him – the Vendée Globe non-stop, singlehanded, round the world race. Discussing the importance of racing from a young age, Golding said: 'If I knew what I know now I would have got involved in the Olympic classes when I was young – this is without question the best

Tips from the top

Dee Caffari MBE

Former school teacher, Dee Caffari, was the first woman to sail single-handed and non-stop around the world in both directions. She also finished sixth overall in the 2008/09 Vendée Globe from a fleet of 30 and, with an all girl crew, smashed the monohull sailing speed record around Britain and Ireland.

Photo – Sue Pelling

Dee's advice on how to become a professional sailor:

- Follow your dreams as you never know where they may take you.
- Sail on as many different types of boats with as many different types of sailors, as you will learn a little from everyone.
- If you truly want to achieve a career in sailing, you need to believe you can do it and stick at it. It may be a struggle at times so you need to be tenacious. If it was easy then everyone would be doing it!

grounding for a pro race sailor. . . Overall – I would not change a thing – I greatly enjoyed all my time in the Fire Service and I still love the sailing I am doing now.'

Dee Caffari also came into the professional racing game after quitting her previous career. Caffari was a secondary school teacher of Physical Education for five years, but always had a desire to work in the marine industry so she qualified as a watersports instructor and worked on charter yachts to gain experience before venturing into the professional sailing world. She said:

> 'I really enjoyed teaching, however, I felt it was the right job too early for me. I still craved adventure and really wanted to travel so I took a leap of faith and decided to leave the profession in my mid-twenties. At that stage I had no idea I would end up where I am now and I have never regretted the decision because it has opened up a whole new world of opportunities for me.

Global sailor Steve White facing the world alone aboard his IMOCA 60 *Toe in the Water.* Photo – Bernard Gergaud.

> Once I had my teaching qualification and some experience under my belt, I felt that it was a career that I could go back to if life on the waves ever came to an end. The biggest step was retraining and being aware that qualifications were just the first stepping stone to a career in the marine industry. Experience counts for so much and you must be prepared to start at the bottom and work your way up.’

Another relative newcomer on the professional round the world circuit is Steve White who got into sailing by accident in 1996, quit his job as a car mechanic, and then went on to complete the 2007/08 Vendée Globe.

> ‘A friend wanted me to tow his 17 ft Lysander to Weymouth because he didn’t have a hitch on his car. I had a quick sail that day, then another sail across Portland Harbour a week later and I really was hooked immediately.

> I think the thing that really inspired me was a trip I took in February 1998 – I sailed to the Fastnet Rock on an ex-BT Global Challenge 67 yacht. It was my first time on a big boat, first experience of bad weather, and my first encounter with professional sailors. I knew instantly that I had found my calling and vowed there and then to sail professionally and to compete in the Vendée Globe.'

Without another thought he handed in his notice with his job restoring classic cars and picked up a job at a local boatyard, and immediately set about getting as much practical experience as possible and his RYA qualifications. He then got a job with Pete Goss (former global racing sailor) working on a racing project he was pursuing at the time, and in 2001 he went to work for Chay Blyth's Challenge Business, where he was charged with training skippers and crews planning on competing in the Global Challenge.

White's method of gaining as much experience as possible is one of the best things he could have done because not only was he earning a small salary for him and his family to live on, he was getting himself known on the circuit. He also managed to record a log of over 1,00,000 miles including 25 roundings of the Fastnet Rock, which was a great achievement to have under his belt.

It wasn't until 2005 however, that White took the plunge and made the final step towards fulfilling his Vendée Globe dream. He handed in his notice at Challenge Business and he and his wife Kim drove to Lymington to secure a charter deal on an Open 50 yacht in which he could compete in the 2005 OSTAR single handed trans-Atlantic race.

Against all odds, White won the 2005 OSTAR from Plymouth to Boston in an old, tired boat in extremely rough conditions. That was his first solo race of any kind, and he was ranked 7th in the world by FICO.

On the back of the OSTAR victory, the Whites secured funding to buy an aging Open 60 but admitted they had a difficult time keeping the campaign going. 'I had to do corporate charters, and ultimately re-mortgaged the house a further three times.'

White explained how positively he felt about switching careers to take up a life in a fairly volatile environment: 'Very positive. You always have to be positive. I did feel a bit daunted as the enormity of the task dawned on me. This happened in cycles really; as you feel you achieved each significant step towards the goal, then the next challenge is revealed, and even more questions and gaps in your knowledge are exposed.'

It is interesting how many of today's professional round the world sailors such as Pete Goss, Mike Golding, Dee Caffari and Steve White, cut their teeth on Global Challenge racing, or have been involved with the company in some way or another. The Global Challenge (formerly British Steel Challenge) was a round the world yacht race (westabout – against prevailing winds and currents) started by Sir Chay Blyth in 1989. The event was held every four years in matching yachts, crewed by ordinary men and women who paid to take part. Lack of sponsorship forced the company into its demise leaving what many describe as a fairly large gap on the professional ladder. Thankfully, the Clipper Round the World race, which works on a similar pay-to-sail format is still running successfully and continues to introduce new sailors into the yacht racing scene (see box on page 115).

White said that the training at Challenge Business was unbelievable, particularly for those new to the sport like himself who wanted to pursue a career in the marine industry: 'If you took on a Challenge employee, then you knew pretty much what you were getting. It is difficult to get into the Volvo Ocean Race, America's Cup and Vendée Globe without a solid grounding in something like that.'

Golding, endorsing this view, said: 'Without any question my biggest break into the professional sailing world was the British Steel Challenge. Without that the rest might have remained a dream.'

Getting yourself known on the professional racing circuit is one of the best ways of marketing yourself. Getting to know what's going on and being in the right place at the right time are also important factors when looking for work in this sector.

As with any professional sailing job, talent is one of the key qualities needed to become a round the world sailor. You also need a positive outlook, strong personality, and shouldn't be afraid of being alone in extreme, dangerous conditions for long periods of time.

In order to make a campaign work and be successful by way of gaining sponsors to help fund it, ideally you should have a good business head, and dealing with people should be second nature. You need to be a good ambassador and always take the time to speak to people because you never know where your next sponsorship deal is coming from. Golding commenting on sponsorships said: 'Sponsorship is essential in a sport where at the top level the boats cost many millions of pounds. In the hardcore professional classes you will not find any privateer entries as you would have 10 years ago. . . It is vital to have a real understanding of why and how sponsors derive their value from their participation with the sport – no sponsor – no sailing!'

Although White says he copes well with the business side of his company he wishes he knew more: 'I now realise that learning how to run a business, and marketing are very important. For me, being a former motor mechanic and learning all about business was by far the biggest learning curve; much bigger than the sailing. Basically if you are thinking about following a similar route to me here are some key pieces of advice: Never give up, make your own luck by working hard and building a good reputation as a worker. Keep your goals, both short and long term, clearly in your mind and the rest will happen.'

Commenting on the likely cost of running a solo round the world campaign, Brian Thompson, leading global skipper said the first thing you need to do is consider the cost of the boat: 'For a competitive second-hand IMOCA 60 you'll be looking at spending 1.5 million Euros, or

Tips from the top

Brian Thompson

Brian Thompson is one of the world's most successful and experienced offshore racers with 25 sailing records, as either skipper or watch captain, under his belt including the non-stop round the world speed sailing record with a time of 58 days, 9 hours, 32 minutes, 45 seconds aboard *Cheyenne* (ex-*PlayStation*) in 2004.

Photo – Sue Pelling

Brian's advice on how to make it, and survive on the professional offshore circuit:

- Make sure you can sail offshore safely on your own – you do need to be a very good seaman, so get yourself a Yachtmaster Certificate and do as many offshore miles as you can. At the same time read as much as possible about the sport.
- Sail with as many good sailors as possible – to improve your all round abilities in all the essential aspects including navigation, tactics, meteorology, steering, sail handling, and boat repair. Make sure you have the skills of a top level fully crewed sailor. You should aim to become the best sailor on every boat you sail on. Try double handed racing next, to continue learning, and to see if you enjoy being on the high seas and having to work much more generally than in a fully crewed boat. Also, if you go as a co-skipper on a double handed boat, you have the advantage of not having to actually purchase a boat initially.
- Then go out and somehow get yourself a Mini Transat, Figaro or Class 40 and race in an established solo class. Despite all the previous training, you will find there will be a whole lot more to learn when you are finally on your own.

3 million Euros for a new one. Then budget 1.5 million Euros to run the team properly each year, and then perhaps as much as the same again can be spent on activation – getting the sponsor the right coverage and fulfilling their hospitality needs.'

Thompson is one of the world's most successful and experienced offshore racers (solo and with a team). He has 25 sailing records as either skipper or watch captain under his belt including the non-stop round the world speed sailing record in 58 days, 9 hours, 32 minutes, 45 seconds aboard *Cheyenne* (ex-*PlayStation*) in 2004 and has put together numerous solo campaigns. He believes going down the budget route initially is not a bad idea:

'In my opinion there is some logic in doing a very low budget Vendée Globe campaign as you immediately become a part of a very well known and marketed event. This can be achieved for something like 400 thousand Euros to buy and refit an old boat, and then 250 thousand Euros to do the event.

However, for the same figures you could do a very decent Class 40 campaign in the Global Ocean Race (GOR), and hope to be at the front of the fleet, rather than inevitably at the back of a Vendée Globe fleet, however well you sail. One could argue that this would be a better way to go, with that same budget.'

What can go wrong

The first thing to consider when thinking about going solo is how you would deal with a situation should your plan to become a professional round the world skipper fail to live up to expectations. Imagine giving up your well-paid job, and remortgaging the house to buy a boat, struggling to find work and eventually losing everything through lack of funds. It is a grim picture to paint but it has to be seriously thought about before you embark on such a campaign.

The second thing to consider is the risk factor of solo sailing, and whether you can deal with being totally self-sufficient. Sailing offshore, miles from anywhere with a crew is risky enough but at least if you do fall overboard, crack your head, cut yourself, or have a serious medical condition, there'll be others around to help deal with the situation. When you are sailing alone, thousands of miles from anywhere, however, there is simply no one to help you should anything go wrong.

One of the biggest challenges you'll face is sleep deprivation and fitness – being able to cope with huge loads such as handling the sails and equipment, and having enough muscle power to cope with hoisting and lowering the sails in all conditions including 70 kt+ storms in the Southern Ocean.

Brian Thompson is one of the world's most successful and experienced offshore racers, yet even someone like him can be tested to the limit in extreme conditions. What happened to him during the 2008/9 Vendée Globe – non-stop singlehanded round the world race aboard the Open 60 *Kingdom of Bahrain*, where he eventually finished fifth overall, was something he confesses to be the nearest he'd ever been to a fatal accident. He basically had a problem with the mainsail getting jammed halfway up the mast, which meant he had to climb the mast to fix it. It was on Christmas Day 2008 in the Southern Ocean off Tasmania after the 85 kt wind had abated enough for him to give it a go.

The ocean can be a lonely, hostile place so you need stamina to be a professional solo sailor. Photo – Mark Lloyd/Lloyd Images.

> 'It was still incredibly windy but I managed to get up there, however, in the extreme conditions all my climbing equipment became tangled up and jammed which meant I couldn't actually get down. I'd also forgotten to take a knife up with me so I couldn't even cut myself down. I was basically being thrown around like a rag doll at the top of the mast getting weaker and weaker and no one knew I was there. Somehow I managed to reconfigure the equipment, untangle it and made my way down after an hour and a half.'

Thompson says that it was one of those incidents that just escalated. What started off as a relatively simple job just evolved into a nightmare, which could so easily have ended tragically. 'Although I did learn lessons from the incident, I don't think any amount of experience would have prepared me for what happened up there.'

In the same race leading French skipper Yann Eliès was seriously injured while in the Southern Ocean 800 miles to the south of Australia. As he was preparing a sail, the yacht came to a violent halt in a wave and he collapsed with a badly fractured femur. He was helpless and spent two days in the cabin of his 20 m (60 ft) yacht *Generali* unable to move because of the excruciating pain, which meant some of the other competitors hundreds of miles away had to divert and risk their lives in an effort to help him. With combined efforts he was eventually rescued and flown to Perth by the Australian Navy.

In a team

Professional sailors who don't like the idea of spending months on end racing around the world non-stop alone, in life threatening conditions, opt for events such as the Volvo Ocean Race (VOR), or the Barcelona World Race (double-handed). These are extremely tough races but do have stopovers around the globe, which allow crews to recover, and in some cases such as the VOR, carry out crew swap overs.

During the nine months of the Volvo Ocean Race for example, each yacht entered has a sailing team of 11 professional crew who race day and night for more than 20 days at a time.

Clipper Round the World Race

One of the most sensible options for anyone with little or no experience of sailing who is considering a career as a professional global sailor, is to sign up for a place on the Clipper Round the World Race run by Clipper Ventures.

This is the only organisation in the world offering the opportunity for non-professionals to compete in a round the world yacht race on a pay-to-sail format.

The company was set up in 1995 by Sir Robin Knox-Johnston – the first man ever to sail solo and non-stop around the world – and in that time has successfully transformed more than 4,000 sailors of 18–70 years old, into racing yachtsmen and women.

Although it will take 11 months to complete, and cost from £8,000 (for one leg) to just over £40,000 for the entire race, you'll be guaranteed a really good grounding in which to base the start of your professional racing career. By the end of the 11-month journey you will have gained so much experience and knowledge because as well as the sailing, you'll become multi-skilled in all sorts of areas that you probably would never have imagined, including plumbing, sorting out the electrics, cleaning, baking, repairing sails, weather forecasting and IT. You might even find yourself becoming a medic. The cost includes all training, food and equipment, and foul-weather gear needed to complete the race.

(*Continued*)

The Clipper Round the World Race will provide a firm platform from which to kick start your professional sailing career. Photo – Clipper Ventures Plc.

This marathon of a race which covers over 40,000 miles, takes place every two years in a fleet of ten identical, state of the art, Tony Castro-designed Clipper 70 yachts. Crews (22 on each yacht) are recruited from all walks of life including taxi drivers, company CEOs, ballet dancers, bankers, nurses, doctors and vets, most of whom have never sailed before.

When you get to the stage of looking for work, it's worth remembering that companies such as Clipper Ventures who not only run the Clipper Round the World Race but also Clipper Events, employ full-time staff to run the business, so it could be worth making contact with them to see what positions are available.

The VOR course, which takes the fleet to the most hostile places on the planet such as the Southern Ocean and round Cape Horn, provides the ultimate challenge for the professional sailor with only the toughest of the tough completing the entire course.

Inshore and offshore racing

Although there are always plenty of racing teams looking for highly experienced crew for inshore and offshore racing yachts and smaller keelboats, forget any idea of just pitching up and expecting to find work. To join a professional racing team you have to have an exceptionally good CV proving you have the talent to make a difference to the performance of the team. You might have a string of RYA exams under your belt but without the experience of high profile racing and the reputation to go with it, you probably won't get too far.

The America's Cup for example employs only the most talented sailors in the world who have usually progressed to that level through Olympic sailing. And the crew at pro race series events such as the Med Cup (annual summer series of events held in TP52/GP42 designed

Professional offshore racing sailor Nick Bubb demonstrates the cramped conditions aboard a 7 m (21 ft) Mini Transat yacht. Photo – Sue Pelling.

Tips from the top

Nigel King

Photo – Sue Pelling

Nigel King is captain and coach for the pro RC44, Team Aqua. He also offers professional sailing services, including coaching, project management, technical advice and consultancy as well as campaigning his own projects such as Figaro sailing.

Nigel's advice on how to make it in the professional yachting world:

- Professionalism, integrity and reliability are three key qualities required to succeed with a career in sailing. It's a very small industry and if you get a bad reputation it can be hard to shake it off.
- Get a reputation for being hardworking, keen to learn and easy to get on with and you will always get invited back.
- Speculate to accumulate, which means there are times when you need to go sailing for free. For example, if you think it will be fun, good for your sailing, or you want to meet a new client then be prepared to put some time in.
- Better to under sell and over achieve.
- Be pro-active. Get yourself out there. You can't just sit there waiting for the phone to ring.

yachts), the RC44 Championship Tour, the World Match Racing Tour, or those who race on race yachts at regattas all round the world, are mainly made up of America's Cup or Olympic class sailors, or those who've already proved themselves in other competitive sectors of the sport.

To become a professional racing sailor therefore, you need to understand that you'll have to put in a lot of work before you'll make the grade as a racer on the pro circuit. And it's not just about sailing. Although you will need to put in plenty of time racing on all sorts of different yachts, it is important to spend as much time as you can learning how yachts work, and how to maintain them. The rig (mast and sails that provide the power), and the systems on most hi-tech racing yachts are extremely complex, so the more you understand how they work, the more chance there is of understanding how to fix them should failures occur while racing.

The same applies if you are thinking about solo sailing in the long term – maybe competing in the Route du Rhum, The Artemis Transat (Singlehanded Transatlantic Race) or the Mini Transat (also known as the Transat 650 this is a solo race in 6.50 m (21 ft) yachts from France to Brazil), spending time working in a boat yard learning about the finer points of yacht maintenance, is essential.

From the age of 14, Nigel King juggled his schooling with working from midnight to 6am every morning at Walthamstow market, and had never stepped foot on a sailing boat until he was 18. He applied the same enthusiasm to his sailing career learning all he could about not only sailing but also maintenance, and skills such as sailmaking. Reminiscing about his first job as a sailing professional, and how he learnt the hard way, King said: 'The first hour of my first real sailing job was a disaster because I dropped a whole bunch of parts from a massive custom winch into the water. I was so scared that I quit on the spot. Fortunately the skipper would not accept my resignation, at least not until I had swam down to retrieve all the bits and put the winch back together!'

King is also someone who firmly believes that being a professional is about much more than just being a good sailor: 'It's more about being an entertainer! There are many out there who are not necessarily the best sailors in the world but what they do is they make sure they deliver to their employers. We're basically in the entertainment business; if the owners are not entertained, then they won't pay the bills.'

Another important aspect to running a solo sailing project is being a good organiser. Miranda Merron, a pro sailor who left her job in advertising to go sailing, and now campaigns a Class 40 yacht said: 'It's a business so you need to be able to do everything including accounts and being good at your own PR. You have to be incredibly adaptable as a solo sailor because you don't have a team to help out. And if you have a sponsor, you have to look after them too.'

Actually earning money in this business, whether it's round the world racing or transatlantic racing, is far from easy, and in most cases, relies on sponsorship. Attracting sponsorship to run a sailing campaign is a challenge in itself but if you have a good business head – or maybe come from a business environment – then you will certainly have an advantage in knowing some of the best companies to go for, and how to pitch yourself correctly.

Ian Williams, talking about whether he feels the experience of his previous legal career has played an important role in the business side of his sailing career, said: 'I think that coming into professional sailing at a later age than many do, has allowed me to take a more mature and consequently more strategic approach to my sailing in terms of where I want my career to go. My legal training helps a bit in certain areas but more I think my previous career has taught me a level of self discipline and also how to act as a professional.'

Tips from the top

Ian Williams

Photo – Charles Anderson/ Performance PR Ltd

Ian Williams is a world class match racing sailor having won the World Match Racing Tour world championship twice. He is also a three times Youth UK Match Racing National Champion and three times Senior UK National Match Racing Champion.

Ian's advice on how to market yourself on the professional circuit:

- You need to think about who you are marketing yourself to then build yourself a profile either through the media or through word of mouth. On the media side, I just tried to do as good a job as possible whenever I did an interview as the more interesting you can be, the more likely it is that the interview will be used. Regarding word of mouth, all you can really do is a good job of the sailing unless you are the sort of person who likes hanging around sailing bars and talking yourself up.
- Direct marketing (or you could call it sales) to a specific person, whether that is the CEO/marketing director of a company, the owner of a boat you want to sail, or a person who is influential in selecting a team.

Making the grade and staying there

Pro sailors like Pete Cumming say that although there is always a certain amount of 'it's who you know rather than what you know', you need to be able to prove yourself to get on in the professional racing circuit.

> 'Those funding projects generally want good results. They firstly fill the key positions on the boat with the best talent they can get hold of and then the key sailors will bring in 'their guys' who they work with on other teams/projects. This forms the old boy network and is why you generally see the same faces on many different boats. This is a hard nut to crack and for sure if you are lucky enough to get into an established team and do a good job they will generally take you with them onto

bigger and better things in the future. Generally the best sailors remain in the sport the longest, a little luck with a few breaks is not a bad thing.'

There is always a high degree of uncertainty with sailing projects so you always need to be striving to produce your very best both onshore and on the race course. The ability to fit into diverse teams and get on with the job in hand is also an important quality. You also need to have a positive outlook and be constantly on the look out for the next project, which means a lot of time will be spent networking. Cumming added: 'If you like to know where your pay cheque is coming from each month then this is not the sport for you. Pro sailing is 50 per cent trying to find work, and 50 per cent sailing.'

Gaining and maintaining a good reputation is the single most important factor to consider. Cumming says that delivering what the owner or sponsor requires is a priority. 'The sailing business, is a small world and a good reputation is key. Reputation is driven by results and what fellow crew think of you and your ability. You have to be both sailor and sports agent to work hard to create the breaks with the big teams. Generally, the bigger the team, the bigger the pay cheque. Like any sport as you work up the ladder, the more work will be offered to you and one drives the other until you are making a very nice living.'

Pro match racer Ian Williams says that you are effectively running a business when you are a professional sailor and business is all about sales. 'If you are good at marketing and selling yourself, you will be successful in the financial sense. There are quite a lot of pro sailors out there who are much better at marketing themselves than they are at sailing.'

'The rest is about simple professionalism as a sportsman. Talent will get you so far, but being a successful professional is mostly about being better prepared than your opposition and performing well even when you do not feel like it.'

Being totally committed is also a key factor that goes into making sailing for a living a success. Some areas of the sector involve being away from home for extended periods of time which means family life can be affected. King says if you have a partner, they have to be extremely understanding. 'Thankfully my wife is understanding. On average I am away on business for over 200 days a year, and have been since we got married. Consequently, when I am home I try to fit into her life and don't expect her routine to change just because I am home. I am also fortunate in the fact that my wife can join me at some of the special locations around the world. It's amazing how a little bribery goes a long way!'

Salaries

Because professional sailing is so unstructured with so many variables it is difficult to give an accurate estimate of the sort of salaries sailors are likely to earn in this sector. Racing for a living is one of the most difficult areas of the sport to earn serious money from, unless of course you are talented enough to make it as a sailor in one of the big sponsored events such as the America's Cup or Volvo Ocean Race, or as an independent solo sailor with a good sponsor.

Ian Williams commenting on pro sailors' salaries says there are a lot of sailors out there making £30–50,000 a year: 'I think a reasonably talented sailor who is willing to put in the time can get there fairly easily. There are some but not many making over £100,000 as it is, of course, much harder to achieve.'

Although Pete Cumming says he agrees it is hard to put a figure on salaries in this sector, he knows what you should be looking for. 'I would say you should look to be pulling in around £40,000–£80,000 if you are part of a good team in a senior position. I also project manage for the sponsor so I am now luckily on the higher end of the pay scale.'

Artemis Offshore Academy

Finding a way onto the professional racing circuit is possibly one of the most difficult challenges to face if you are considering going sailing for a living. Even some of the country's most talented sailors who have spent a lifetime racing and training, fail to 'make it' and eventually slip away off the scene. This is generally not through lack of racing skill but more usually through lack of funds and sponsorship.

Recognising the need to help capture and develop British talent, Artemis Ocean Racing launched the Artemis Offshore Academy, which is aimed specifically at developing British solo talent on the international racing scene.

This is a fantastic step forward for the future of British offshore racing success because it means that anyone who already has the right skill and needs support and a structure in which to progress can apply to the academy to be considered for the squad.

So, if you think you have what it takes to be considered for a place on the squad, have a look on the website: artemisoceanracing.com/academy.

Chapter 6

Expedition yacht work

Expedition yachts – those that venture to far-flung atolls, the Great Capes or frozen high latitudes – require highly experienced crew because of the specialist nature of the job. Some vessels such as the Dutch Sail Training Ship *Europa*, or *Pelagic Australis* – Skip Novak's famous 22 m (74 ft) polar expedition yacht – stock up with supplies and head south like migrating birds to spend the season undertaking expeditions in Antarctica's summer.

While travelling by sea on an expedition yacht to the Antarctic or the Arctic for example must rate as one of the ultimate, and most rewarding voyages with a chance to experience nature at the extreme, it goes without saying, it is also one of the most demanding and potentially dangerous jobs because not only will you be working in continuous sub-zero conditions, you'll also be away from civilisation for long periods of time which means if anything does go wrong, the chances of survival are dramatically reduced.

With this in mind it goes without saying that gaining experience by spending a couple of seasons toughening yourself up, and training for your exams will take priority. One idea is to

Europa's crew enjoys one of the more pleasant days in Antarctica. Photo – Hajo Olij.

get involved as a trainee aboard a sail training ship such as *Europa*. Klaas Gaastra, the skipper, says the ship takes 40 trainees per trip. Although you will be fare paying, you will get plenty of hands-on experience such as acting as iceberg 'look out' on the foredeck at night. This will give you an idea of whether or not this is the sort of work you'd consider undertaking in the future. On a ship like *Europa*, there are 14 professional crew members who run the ship, including guides who specialise in the flora, fauna and wildlife of the Polar regions who work alongside the trainees. This means if you are serious about expedition sailing, there are openings available.

Stuart Richardson who originally worked in the finance sector in London became skipper of the expedition yacht *Pelagic Australis* for four years. However, it wasn't a job he just stepped into. He spent many years after his City career enhancing his CV, and was fortunate to have plenty of previous sailing experience. Richardson was chosen as a race skipper at Challenge Business (the company that used to specialise in pay-to-sail round the world races).

Richardson described the qualities required to take a role as a crew member on an expedition yacht: 'Most of the skippers on these sort of yachts have either come from a racing route or have been fishermen. Ocean Racing teaches you lots of good stuff for expedition sailing. The racing gives you the sailing skills you need to get around but in the South the main focus really is on getting from A to B safely.'

According to Richardson, most crew start off by working as a volunteer for two or three years. They live on the boat and are fed and watered but not paid: 'All the crew I employed were sailors who I met down South who had either hitched rides on yachts from New Zealand or got there other ways. After a while they build a reputation and you have to hire them. I guess it's a bit like dock walking in the Med. We only hired people on this basis. I get CVs all the time from people with no experience of the South who want to go there, but experience in the sort of conditions they are likely to encounter is a priority.'

As well as being an exceptionally skilled yachtsman, and someone who can cope with extreme conditions, you have to be a good manager too and be able to face dangerous situations head on, with no support. When you are down in the Antarctic for example, the nearest land mass is Cape Horn and South America. You have to be a sound communicator, speaking Spanish and French also helps a lot and above anything, be a skilled engineer.

Richardson said engineering qualities are extremely important: 'If you bend a prop blade on ice in most parts of the world, a telephone call later a diver will arrive and change it for you, or perhaps you may have to dive to do it. But in the South, the only way you will get it changed is to do it yourself, and cold water diving, in drysuits is another skill entirely.'

Picking up an expedition sailing type job, therefore, will require certain skills and you probably won't see too many of these types of jobs advertised. Getting a job skippering such a yacht will, in most cases, be down to reputation and good references, and as mentioned before, being in the right place at the right time. Richardson, commenting on how he secured his job as skipper of *Pelagic Australis* said:

> 'Interestingly, the reason I switched to expedition sailing was simple; I was approached out of the blue by Skip Novak who asked If I fancied giving it a go.
>
> I guess the reason I was asked was largely down to my reputation as a sailor with Challenge Business. The role as skipper on *Pelagic Australis* was simply to try and help the client achieve their objectives. Whether it was filming wildlife, making documentaries, or taking climbers and ski teams to remote locations, didn't really matter, they all wanted to go further south than anyone else, to see things that have never been seen before, and to take risks. Our job therefore, was to deliver those demands and manage the risk.'

Although Richardson says there are many good points about this sort of work including building up strong friendships with fellow crew members, and going to some of the most amazing places on earth, there are plenty of downsides. 'I suppose the worst aspect however, is the fact you never really get any time off. It's 24/7/365. We would join in Cape Town in September and finish in Cape Town in July, so that is particularly tough.

When you are fortunate enough to work on a yacht in Antarctica, anything else – any other job – seems very tame, boring and easy, but there comes a time when you need to come back to the temperate latitudes, get a bit of vitamin D, cash in on the experience and be nearer home.'

Expedition sailing is not just confined to the extreme north and south, there are plenty of other opportunities to bag a job on an expedition yacht in other parts of the globe including the UK on scientific research yachts in the Hebrides, or further afield such as the Pacific, Mediterranean, the Baltic, New Zealand, Australia and parts of Africa. Many of these yachts (both power and sail) take paying charter guests, and volunteers who are keen to gain experience in this sort of work. However, they also need crew to run the yachts, so if you have an interest in adventure sailing, make contact with some of the companies that run these expeditions and find out what they are looking for when employing staff.

Chapter 7
Sailing support jobs

While sailing, teaching, working on yachts, and delivering yachts makes up a huge part of the marine industry; the biggest by far is the support sector, which acts as a foundation for the entire sport and industry. The variety of jobs that go into supporting the marine industry is vast which means whatever career you've come from, there's every chance you'll find your skills are transferable to a new career in this part of the industry.

As well as boatbuilders, sailmakers, yacht surveyors, mast makers, and numerous other skilled jobs, there are the supporting organisations such as the Royal Yachting Association (RYA), the British Marine Federation (BMF), and the International Sailing Federation (ISAF) employing hundreds of staff in all number of different sailing related jobs. From finance and data control to RIB driving and running sailing events, the skills required are endless which means it could be worth investigating what options are available.

The loft at Elvström Sails provides a light and spacious working environment for designers, cutters and machinists. Photo – Elvström Sails.

The charitable sector too, including organisations such as the RNLI and the Ellen MacArthur Cancer Trust, do rely heavily on voluntary work, but there are also full-time salaried jobs available in managerial and admin roles, which means that those with experience in the charity field could be well placed to exploit their knowledge in a career in this area.

If you have a passion for yacht racing maybe something to consider is event management. Most of the high profile, sponsored events such as the Artemis Transat, or the Extreme Sailing Series, are run by professional companies such as OC Group who are experienced in these sorts of specialist sports. As well as the logistics and management side of companies, there are numerous other openings that could require skills you may already have including IT, database management systems, or finance control. The opportunities are endless, which means you need to do a lot of research into the sort of jobs available before pitching yourself into the market.

The British **sailmaking** industry is one area to consider if you are a keen sailor and are willing to learn more about the technicalities of sail power. Salesmen, designers, production specialists,

Sailmaker at North Sails UK loft in the machine pit in the final stages of completing a suit of sails. Photo – Richard Langdon/Ocean Images.

plotter operators, seamers, sailmakers, and hand workers are all roles to consider in the sailmaking industry. However, it is worth bearing in mind that in some areas such as design, which are specialised, it will probably be extremely difficult to make a transition into the industry unless you have an engineering background, wind tunnel work or plotter skills.

Neil Mackley who is responsible for sales and marketing at North Sails UK says although there are those who specialise in design, there are plenty of other jobs that are equally important: 'The guys and girls on the loft floor play key roles in a manufacturing team. Most of the components are now pre made, so the sailmaker is more of a case of putting the various components into the sail.'

Being honest about sailmaking as a career, Mackley commented:

'It can be a great lifestyle if you get involved with boat programmes and oversee the development process of new sails. The loft floor guys are needed as they form the production team, but the sales and design side has lots of opportunity. My old contract stated: '. . . and we like you to be involved in as much sailing as you can stand.' Although endless sailing sounds wonderful, it's not quite the same when you do it for a living!

So would I recommend it? If you think you have what it takes to work long hours doing a job/hobby you love then it's a great lifestyle, especially if you're single!'

According to Mackley there are no set figures for the sort of salary you could earn but generally those working on the loft floor could expect to receive between £15–25,000 per year. 'The guys who own the most are the ones that get headhunted to go and work for the big America's Cup campaigns and become part of the America's Cup team.'

Giving up a high-powered job in the City to become a **boatbuilder** doesn't sound like a natural step, yet according to Jonathan Richardson – Manager at the International Boatbuilding Training College (IBTC) in Lowestoft, Suffolk – a high proportion of students signing up for boatbuilding courses come from that sector. Richardson believes that although boatbuilding is a manual job there's a lot of brainpower needed too, which is what he thinks attracts people to the profession. 'I believe it is the perfect combination between using your head and using your hands, and at the end of the day a woodworker has something to show for it. Even if the students go back to their original job and join the rat race again on a part time basis after they have completed the course, many of them use boatbuilding as their way of staying sane.'

Even if you have never had any experience of boats or woodwork, it is possible to become a boatbuilder at any age but you need to invest time and money in order to obtain a good education. There are several colleges in the UK specialising in boatbuilding including IBTC in Lowestoft, and the Boatbuilding Academy in Lyme Regis. These generally teach traditional methods, which give a good grounding and are highly recommended should you wish to become a skilled boat-builder, or want to investigate other areas of the industry such as project management in the superyacht sector. Richardson from IBTC says once you learn the traditional methods it is easy to transfer the skills over to more modern methods: 'We have a number of new builds and a lot of restoration projects on the go, about 30 on the go at one time, which gives our students so much hands-on experience. For those who want to learn about glassfibre and other methods we have courses for them too.'

So how much would it cost to train to be a boatbuilder and what qualifications do you get? To train for a year, which is effectively a 47-week course, for a Practical Boatbuilding Diploma at IBTC, the fee is approximately £11,000 but there are grants available, which means it is possible to get a sizeable chunk of your fees paid. The college will provide advice on the best way of going about applying for a grant.

Boatbuilder at Petticrows puts the final touches on a brand-new International Dragon. Photo – Sue Pelling.

Ailsa Spindler who is in her mid-fifties decided to quit the rat race and give up a senior managerial position in the City to train to become a boatbuilder. She knew a bit about boats, and woodwork and eventually made the boat/woodworking connection and investigated the options.

> 'I was blown away with the college in Lowestoft. It is unbelievable because you have the opportunity to work on big boats of 50 ft plus, as well as smaller craft. There's such a huge variety and it is so professional, and the quality of training is so high. Everyone does 12 weeks of joinery before they are let loose on the boats. You basically have to reach a standard before moving on which means the quality of workmanship is top class and something you can be proud of.
>
> The other thing that impressed me was the fact it is run like a proper boat yard which means you have to clock in at 0800. It is a bit of a challenge but it's done for a purpose to prepare you for the real world and enable you to have a whole set of skills including understanding you have to work to a schedule to meet targets.'

Having completed her course, Spindler decided to go it alone and set up her own business/workshop in Bulgaria because she felt there were many openings for skilled woodworkers there. 'There is so much potential in the Black Sea marine areas and the Danube where there are some seriously big boats, so I will be looking for boat building/restoring opportunities. In places like Bulgaria you can see people still have a tradition of mending things rather than the throw away societies we are more used to. I think some of the lesser developed countries have a healthier attitude towards hand skills so I thought it would be worth a try.'

There is a huge market for skilled woodworkers in the marine industry but you have to decide in which area to specialise once you've learnt the basic skills. You might find you prefer to work with more modern methods including glass/carbonfibre, in which case you should do plenty of research, find a boatyard, and have a chat to them about the sort of positions available. Most of the high-performance race boats built in this country at places like Neville Hutton Boatbuilders in Lymington, which specialises in large racing yachts, or Petticrows in Burnham-on-Crouch that build world class Dragons for example, employ specialists who work with hi-tech materials. You'll probably also find those who work there will have come from a strong sailing background with plenty of experience, but it is always worthwhile making contact with companies like these just in case there's an opening available.

Ipswich-based Spirit Yachts has built up a reputation of producing some of the world's best custom-designed and built, elegant, contemporary modern classic yachts ranging from pocket cruisers to superyachts. The company even supplied the 26 m (54 ft) yacht for Bond movie Casino Royale, which appeared in the Venice scene with Daniel Craig as James Bond sitting in a rather relaxed, business-like pose on the bow. This company, which has 30 full-time employees, most of whom are boatbuilders, is run by Sean McMillan, the managing director and senior designer. He has a clear view that in order to become a boatbuilder you need to be sure about the reasons behind why you are doing it. He says that if it is for a fulfilling career with huge job satisfaction and mediocre remuneration, then this could be a good option, however if it is for any other reason then think twice:

> 'If they have genuine talent and are not interested in being particularly wealthy, then they should go ahead. It doesn't pay well, but the rewards in terms of job satisfaction are immense. All that being said, if (as often happens) people want to go into boat building for some kind of religious experience to get over a midlife crisis, we certainly wouldn't take them on. When we are looking to employ new staff they have to have proven skills even if not too much experience. We also look for those with a questioning mind, and a pair of hands that can create what they envisage. Intelligence and a sense of humour are also important because they have to work as part of a very tight team, so prima donnas are out.'

Skilled woodworkers in the new build sector are sought after, but there are other areas to consider including restoration and yacht repair. There are hundreds of boatyards in the UK and worldwide keen to track down those with skill in traditional craft. The National Maritime Museum Cornwall, which has a continuous flow of exhibits passing through its doors, often in a poor state of repair, is one of many examples to consider.

If you have a surveying background then you might consider **yacht surveying** as an option. To qualify as a yacht surveyor however, you certainly need to know about boats, and put some time aside to do a yacht surveying course in order to prepare yourself for surveying exams.

Before you contemplate giving up one career for a life on the road surveying yachts, you should assess whether you have what it takes. Knowing about boats is a priority, and being physically fit enough to climb on and off boats and agile enough to worm your way down into the bilges are important aspects to consider. Ian Nicolson who has been surveying yachts for over 40 years is one of the most respected in the industry. He has written books on the subject and says yacht surveying is far more challenging than being a house surveyor. 'To be a yacht surveyor you need to be tough and be prepared to share bilge space with the odd rat. The hours are also exceedingly long. I've often spent eight hour stints in blizzard conditions in Scotland carrying out a survey.'

To become a yacht surveyor you need to apply to colleges that specialise in marine survey such as Lloyds Maritime Academy, or the International Institute of Marine Surveying (IIMS), where you'll be given advice on the degree course. Nicolson continued: 'Before you even consider signing up you really have got to know your stem from your masthead because otherwise you will

Yacht surveying is a good option if you don't mind working in all conditions. Photo – Sue Pelling.

struggle to keep up. You also need to be articulate, and have enough writing skills to be able to present a professional report to the owner of the yacht, following the survey.'

Building a reputation as a trusted surveyor like Nicolson takes years to achieve and even then you won't make a big living from it. Yacht surveying part-time is another option to consider, especially when you are first setting up. This will allow you to retain the job you already have and start to build up a name for yourself in the industry. Although marketing through advertisements, and PR will be an important factor when building up your business, it will be recommendations as a reliable, trustworthy surveyor that will ultimately be the biggest business provider.

When Steve Harris from the East Coast retired as a Police Marine Officer he decided to turn his passion for sailing into a part time career as a yacht surveyor. He spent a lot of time building up his business and working hard on a job he thoroughly enjoyed but was disappointed that regulations and insurance costs forced him to rethink his surveying business.

> 'I would highly recommend it because if, like me, you have been involved in yachts all your life and have a lot of experience and knowledge, there couldn't be a better option. However, I would like to make others aware that if you are thinking about working alone, on a part time basis, the cost of indemnity insurance to cover liability is so high that it probably wouldn't be worth your while. If you are taking it on as a serious, full time career however, then covering the costs won't be such an issue, but part time, as far as I'm concerned, is not worthwhile.'

An area of the industry that has a shortage of skilled workers and therefore offers relatively good rates of pay is in **mechanics or electrics**. Anyone who has the skills to mend and install electric instruments on yachts is sought after. Maybe you already have a background in this field and wish to expand your knowledge into the marine sector, or are willing to train, either way this is a good option to consider (see superyacht section).

If you have a background in architecture, the **yacht design** route could be worth considering but even with the necessary qualifications and experience in the sailing field, making a living as a yacht designer is a tough option. Mark Mills who runs Mills Design which specialise in the design of innovative performance yachts, says building a career in yacht design particularly in the early stages is incredibly difficult because if you have no track record or no success, what would make someone spend a minimum of £100,000 on something that's unproven, just because you tell them you can do it? 'Even if you are extremely fortunate enough to get on the ladder with a successful design, you still have to convince the next person the yacht you design will be a success. The bottom line is, if you muck up the first time, when you effectively have no firm basis whatsoever, you're basically finished!'

If you are interested in designing racing yachts it is imperative to spend plenty of time on the race circuit sailing as many different types of boats as you can. You also need to spend time learning about yacht maintenance and all the systems that help make yachts function, so find a job and do some labouring for a race team or boat yard.

You'll also need qualifications so sign up for a naval architecture or yacht design course at one of the many on offer in the UK including Southampton University, Southampton Solent University, Strathclyde and Newcastle. In theory it would be beneficial to spend some time doing work experience in a design office to get an idea of what the job is really like, but as Allen Clarke at the Owen Clarke Design Group indicated, in practice, it is incredibly difficult to get a foot in the door of any yacht design company, large or small.

Clarke's advice is to get some work for some of the top flight sailing teams to get an understanding of what makes sailing yachts really tick:

> 'At least you will likely be paid a pittance wage if you are practical and prepared to knuckle down doing the bottom of the food chain job. From there, take what you have learnt and sell yourself to a design office. When applying for positions that don't exist, sell your key skills and tell them how much you have sailed and what sailing you intend to do and just get across how passionate you are about the industry. You will almost certainly have to start at the bottom and work for free to prove yourself. You may be lucky and be in the right place at the right time. If you are good at networking, go to every event you can think of and be seen, sail on all types of yachts from deliveries to events like the ARC, and any of the ocean racing classics. If classic yachts are your thing, then do the classic yacht circuit, offer yourself up as free crew.'

Being patient, diplomatic, having a good understanding for client needs, and the ability to turn a client's requirements into what they want, and not what you want are some of the most important qualities to understand before embarking on a yacht design career.

Key pieces of advice on applying for a design job from Allen Clarke – designer of some of the most high performance racing yachts in the world: 'I have lost count of the number of CVs I have seen at this office, whether young or more mature, in which the prospective candidates fail to get across their sailing experience and capabilities, and also fail to actually do their homework and research what the company they are applying to, really does. Typically being able to carry out either subcontracted CAD (computer-aided design) work or being able to offer rendered images might get you a break but be aware designers seldom like to give up their secrets.'

Most yacht designers will agree that making a name for yourself as a designer in the sailing world is all about multiple career breaks, or having one real big one. Allen Clarke recalling his earliest career breaks remembered when he was setting out: 'Meeting Merfyn Owen (my business partner) when I was in my twenties, and building our first project a 35 ft trimaran *Fiery Cross*, and then sailing it across the Atlantic. The biggest break for Owen Clarke Design however, came in 1999 when a young girl called Ellen MacArthur and her then business partner Mark Turner placed a huge amount of faith in us to run the design team for the *Kingfisher* Open 60 monohull project for the Vendée Globe race. The rest as they say is history.'

There is a growing demand for **meteorologists and forecasters** who not only specialise in marine forecasting for events or record attempts, but also weather routing particularly on the professional racing circuit. This means if you are a competent, competitive racer who has spent a lot of time racing in all conditions, have a firm grip on the understanding of weather, and have an ability to communicate well, this could be an option to consider.

The work of a weather router involves delivering weather and sea information to help provide a tactical advantage over other competitors through optimised route recommendations.

A meteorologist or forecaster plays an important role in ensuring the success of an event. You will usually find that most of the larger regattas such as Cowes Week or Round the Island Race employs a meteorologist to assist not only the race organisers with the weather forecasts for the duration of the event, but also the competitors. With up to 2,000 yachts taking part in the one-day, 50 mile Round the Island Race, the weather forecaster is able to offer the best up to the minute advice about what the weather is likely to do during the race.

Mike Broughton is the managing director of the weather forecasting company winnningwinds.com, which specialises in sailing. Broughton's work involves forecasting for a wide variety of sailors including Olympic medallists and round the world sailors. He also assists in forecasting for race organisers such as the Royal Ocean Racing Club and the America's Cup.

As well as a racing navigator and skipper, and a qualified Master to captain superyachts, up to 3,000 tonnes, Broughton's former career was in the Royal Navy, where he enjoyed a variety of jobs including driving ships and being a 'special forces' Commando helicopter pilot. Using what he learnt during his Naval aviation career, Broughton was able to transfer his forecasting skills to the sport that was close to his heart and now enjoys working as a forecaster.

Broughton says previous sailing experience and having a firm understanding of the conditions is more important than anything:

> 'Understanding what 35 knots of wind against four knots of current really feels like is important and something a forecaster who hasn't spent very much time at sea will struggle with.
>
> My advice for anyone wanting to go down the forecasters route would be to get out and navigate on race boats, have a good understanding of physics and think strategic to tactical when it comes to forecasting. Finally, don't sit on the fence like they teach trainee forecasters, but tell it how you really think it is.'

The ultimate success of major events including round the world races, or solo record attempts relies heavily on the strength of the **sailing support teams**. The organisers are responsible for running events and making sure all components are in place, which means ensuring the right people are employed to carry out the numerous tasks. At global ocean races such as the Vendée Globe, or the Clipper Round the World Race for example – the non-stop, singlehanded round the world race – the organisers will run the event, but the competitors, most of whom will be sponsored, will bring their own support team to ensure their campaign is run as professionally as possible. As well as the sailing team that run, maintain and deliver the yacht to the start port or to wherever it needs to be, there'll be a communications manager who deals with all issues arising in the first instance. Depending on the size of the sponsorship there's likely to be a media manager and a selection of assistants to help out with media events, and someone to look after guests and logistics, although some of these may be brought in on a temporary basis for the duration of an event.

Helen King, whose previous job list includes working at the Tax Office, Ford car dealership, Budget Rent-A-Car and the Ministry of Defence, decided when she was 27 years old, to get out of London and take a job in Salcombe working as manager (on the domestic side) aboard *Egremont* the sailing base at the Island Cruising Club. She then worked for the Forestry Commission in the New Forest and the Coastguard Agency.

A desire to become more involved with the marine industry however, led her to apply for a job advertised in her local newspaper. It was to work for OC Group (Offshore Challenges) a company originally set up by Mark Turner and Dame Ellen MacArthur specialising in sponsorship marketing, communications, and event management. 'It was a tiny advert that said 'interested in Sailing, assistant required for sailing project' . . . The job was very unspecific in terms of the fact they just needed someone to come and be a 'jack of all trades and a master of none.' The money was poor but I took the job nevertheless.'

For King, getting her foot in the door of probably one of the most well-known and respected companies such as Offshore Challenges was one of the best things she could have done because she learned a lot about the running of the professional side of the industry. She was there for five years and having started at the company with an unspecific role, she progressed to General Manager as well as looking after the Offshore Challenges skippers and the projects they were undertaking. 'The job was exciting and interesting because it was so varied. I worked on the office management side, HR, IT support, as well as being PA to the skippers, a shore team coordinator, confidant to Ellen MacArthur, Mark Turner – Ellen's business partner – and global racer Nick Moloney. I learnt a lot particularly from Mark Turner and this was helped by the fact that I was really ready to learn and take on anything that came my way.'

Supporting skippers during the lead up to, and during a race/record attempt sounds like a dream job, and in many ways it is because you are effectively part of the process that makes these professional sailors' dreams come true. You get to work with some of the most talented sailors in the world and build up a special rapport with them. Because you become so close and attached and understand their feelings and emotions, there are times when this sort of job is one of the most difficult. King, talking about her experiences working with Ellen MacArthur and Nick Moloney says because of this it can be incredibly stressful.

> 'Some of the most memorable occasions include the time when Ellen's EPIRB (Emergency Position Indicating Radio Beacon) went off during the Route du Rhum race. I received the initial call from the coastguard. It was very disturbing because it took us a while to get through to her to find out she was okay.
>
> The worst ones I think involved Nick Moloney, which included the time he was caught in a huge storm in the Vendée Globe. He was terrified, and we were up all night trying to help him through it. I had the role of speaking to his family throughout and then letting them know when he was safe and out of danger.
>
> Psychologically this is tough for a skipper which means you have to have the ability to move on very quickly but also allow them enough time to download everything that is on their mind. The other big event for Nick was losing his keel in the Vendée Globe. This was a very concerning time because his life was at risk and my role was to talk to him and to try and find the right words to console him throughout while waiting for the Brazilian Navy to turn up to rescue him.'

As with most jobs in the marine industry, testing times are balanced out by amazing moments. Ellen MacArthur's Vendée Globe finish and Nick Moloney's Jules Verne finish were King's biggest career highlights: 'Being alongside both boats as they crossed the finish line and knowing I was part of that team 'living the dream and all that' was very emotional and I loved it.'

After she left Offshore Challenges King went freelance and became more of a Project Manager working on projects such as Ellen MacArthur's visit to South Georgia, and numerous other high profile events through Into the Blue marketing and PR, including the Extreme 40 campaign for double gold medallist Shirley Robertson OBE, and the race communications side of Mike Golding's Vendée Globe Race. Continuing her exciting career, King was invited to join the Ellen MacArthur Foundation to help set it up. 'I used a lot of the experience I gained through working for OC in terms of managing the company/charity and developing processes, built database and systems, built website, helped on recruitment and all legal and financial matters.'

King offering advice about following a similar career concluded:

> 'I would probably suggest being more focused than I was in terms of what you want to achieve, and work out if lifestyle or money is a priority. Also be absolutely sure you want to work at your hobby. For example, I see sailing as my job, so the last thing I want to do in down time is go sailing. Most people are really surprised by that.

Although qualifications open doors, I would say that having the right personality for this sort of job is really important. Being a member of a shore team for a global skipper/team you almost need to allow it to take over your life – you live and breathe every moment with the skippers especially the single handed sailors. These jobs are not 9-5 and can be demanding, emotional and frustrating, so a good sense of humour is always required, and the ability to survive on little sleep is a necessity.'

If you have engineering or a design background, then one of the most interesting areas of the industry to get involved in is **spar/mast making**. The UK is one of the world leaders in the design and development of spars, which means there are plenty of job opportunities for talented craftsmen. Over the last 20 years the use of carbon fibre for spar making for racing yachts has progressed to the level that the demand for alloy, as a once popular material, is now significantly reduced. Specialists in the carbon fibre field, therefore, are always sought after.

With a turnover of 40 million Euros and employing over 200 staff, the Swedish company Seldén is one of the largest spar manufacturers in the world. A lot of the development takes place at the company's production facilities in the UK, which means there are job opportunities for talented staff who are keen to exploit their engineering or design skills. The same goes for other spar manufactures such as, Z Spar, Eurospar, and Superspar, and so the advice is, carry out plenty of research in the spar making industry,

A mast maker at Seldén prepares the mandrel for a carbon fibre mast, by applying release polish. Photo – Seldén Mast.

decide in which area you would prefer to specialise – dinghy/small keelboats, racing yachts, or cruisers – and investigate the opportunities. As well as all the large manufacturing companies, there are plenty of independent mast makers mostly specialising in carbon fibre, such as Chipstow Boatyard and Aardvark Technologies.

Seldén employ 53 staff in various roles including accountants, sales staff, purchasing and marketing staff, designers, assemblers, riggers [see rigger information below], welders, and those who specialise in pre-preg composites such as carbon fibre. However, according to Steve Norbury – Managing Director of Seldén UK – good engineers with sailing experience who are interested in composite and aluminium construction are the ones always in short supply.

'When we employ staff who are actually involved in the mast making process we tend to look for those who have some kind of experience of masts who maybe have a degree in structural engineering. The skills required do vary however. Making alloy masts is quite hard, physical work, whereas making composite a lot more skill and precision is involved which means a lot more knowledge of the process of laminating is required.'

If you know your mast step from your masthead, and know the purpose of spreaders and stays, then becoming a skilled **rigger**, who are very much in demand, could be a career to consider. The job of a rigger is labour intensive because it involves the fitting out, and setting up of a mast either in the manufacturing process, or during annual yacht re-fits. Rigging is the term used for all the wires and rope work that supports the mast once it's positioned in the yacht, and the term 'rig' is often used to identify the entire set up including the mast, wires, ropes and all the fittings.

As well as all the boat yards around the coast, and mast making companies that require professional riggers to work on a full time basis, there are opportunities to become a self-employed rigger by setting up on your own. The chances of either option turning you into a millionaire are slim but in the right environment where business is constant, there's no reason why you shouldn't make a decent living as a full-time rigger, and enjoy a happy, fulfilling lifestyle effectively playing with boats.

Ian Simons who's been in the rigging industry for over 25 years since he left school says there's no reason why anyone with an interest in boats and who is keen to learn, shouldn't consider becoming a rigger.

'It is the sort of job you learn as you go. There are courses in ropework you can take, and if you want to go down the design route then you'll need to take courses, but generally for a boatyard rigger it is about experience. If you want to work on rigging yachts it does help to understand the mechanics of sailing, so therefore being a sailor does make it a lot easier. My advice is to get out there, sail as many boats as you can because you need to know about what's happening and how the rig will work when under sail power. Talk to people about their rigs and always be willing to learn new things. Rigging is a career where you never stop learning mainly because the technology is moving on all the time.'

Rice & Cole boatyard in Burnham-on-Crouch where Simons works is a relatively small yard handling boats up to 13 m (40 ft), and occasionally bigger. There's a mix of racing and cruising boats which provides plenty of variety, and in a busy period during launching at the beginning of the season, or bringing the boats out of the water for winter lay-up at the end of the season. Simons says it is not unusual to handle the rigging process of up to five yachts a day which equates to about 10-hour days. 'From late February to early March through to June is a particularly busy time for us. Once the boats are off the water there's still plenty to do including servicing all the mooring lines and replacing the ropes. We are working in all elements come rain, shine, frost or snow. Wind is a big problem and

During the process of making a carbon fibre mast, the mast maker is in full charge of the sophisticated machinery. Photo – Seldén Mast.

there are times when it's too windy for working up the top of a mast, but generally you just keep going whatever the weather.'

As well as having a good head for heights when you are working at the top of the mast, and being tough enough to work in all conditions, you'll need to have a creative flair too because the role of a rigger involves being able to learn enough to carry out rig securing/finishing methods such as roll swaging, taluriting (connecting terminal fittings on to wire by squeezing them under high pressure), and hand splicing in wire or rope.

Once you become a skilled rigger there are opportunities to use your experience in other areas such as the building trade. Many a yacht rigger like Simons uses their skill to diversify into other areas such as architectural rigging and balustrading. You also find a lot of mast rigging companies

You will need a good head for heights if you want to become a rigger. Photo – Sue Pelling.

are starting to enter this area because there is a growing demand for skilled riggers to carry out safe constructions. Simons concluded: 'I don't do much of this type of work but it's worth bearing in mind that there are all sorts of construction and development projects in the building industry where you can use your rigging skills.'

Managing a **boat yard** sounds like a dream job if sailing is your passion but, like most jobs in the marine industry, if you turn your hobby into your career you'll probably find you'll be able to write the number of days you actually spend sailing, on the back of a stamp. Regardless of the size of the yard, it will need to be open for business most of the time, to allow those who keep their boats there, the use of the basic facilities.

If it is a big yard like Elephant Boat Yard on the River Hamble, which, in addition to its service facilities, specialises in building quality, custom yachts ranging in size from 8 m (24 ft) to

Working in a boat yard offers a variety of jobs including yacht maintenance. Photo – Sue Pelling.

24 m (72 ft), as well as carrying out major refits and repair work including engine installations, and repaint jobs, it won't be unusual to find at least ten staff employed on a full-time basis. Most of the staff however, are qualified shipwrights and according to Brian Crawley – Elephant Boat Yard's General Manager – it would be extremely rare to employ anyone without boatbuilding skills. 'It is difficult to come into this industry with no skills because you'll end up with an extremely mundane job and will be paid a pittance. We have the odd opening for boat yard labour but generally the only openings we have are for skilled craftsmen, and these are becoming harder and harder to find.' (See boatbuilding on page 130).

A boat sales qualification introduced by the Boat Retailers and Brokers Association (BRBA) and the Association of Brokers and Yacht Agents (ABYA), and supported by the British Marine Federation (BMF) to promote best practice in the industry, means there is more of a career structure for those pursuing a career as a **yacht broker**. This means that although it is still possible to enter the brokerage industry with experience and no qualifications, the boat sales qualification will become increasingly more relevant. For this exam, candidates will need to have at least 12 months' experience as a broker or boat retailer, and have an RYA or equivalent certificate for boat handling for the specific type of boat they are hoping to sell.

Tony Mereweather – Director of Clarke & Carter, the east coast based broker company – says the qualification is a great idea once you've got some experience in the field, but it is possible to become a broker without any prior experience in the broking industry. 'What you do need is to have knowledge of yachts, and to get as much experience of different types of yachts as possible because the bottom line is, you are going to have to sell them. You also need to have certain other qualities including being able to communicate well, to be a good salesman, and most importantly you need to have a good business head.'

Ideally, anyone looking at the broking industry as a career should, rather than setting up on their own, go and work at a brokerage company to gain experience and find out if they enjoy working in that role. You'll also find a lot of companies sign up staff on a part-time basis as seasonal workers in the spring time for example, not just for broking but working in the boat yard. 'The Spring is very busy because all the boats we've sold from about November time onwards, need preparing and valeting for delivery.'

A yacht broker's work doesn't just stop at selling boats, they have to sell the whole concept, in fact because yacht brokers are effectively 'middlemen' they are brokers in many areas. 'When we sell a boat we can end up arranging finance, insurance, negotiating with the yard to do the launching and doing all the work that is involved with that. We are brokers in many areas and I suppose that is what makes it interesting.'

Yacht broking in the superyacht world is another area to consider with companies such as Burgess, Edmiston & Company, and Camper & Nicholsons among those at the top end of the market in the UK. These companies specialise in the sale, purchase, charter, technical service, marketing and management of the finest yachts in the world and are always keen to recruit professionals with transferable skills that could benefit the industry. Rory Boyle – naval architect at Burgess – commenting on the sort of staff they look for said: 'Although we don't have a huge staff turnaround at our London-based office, we are always interested to talk to professionals such as lawyers or city traders who could utilise their skills in the superyacht sector.'

If getting cold and wet working outside in a boatyard fails to appeal to you, you might consider the **sailing clothing manufacturing** business, which covers design, development and many other aspects that could involve transferable skills you may already have. Some of the large British manufacturing companies such as Musto, Gill and Henri Lloyd are world leaders in the field, which means the quality of staff they employ are highly skilled in all aspects including marketing, sales, finance, design and development, and general business administration.

One of the most important aspects of a pioneering company producing specialist products is the power of the evaluation and development team who help the company come up with the ultimate products through stringent testing processes. Nick Gill – MD of Gill – says the company chooses top sailors from a variety of disciplines (dinghy and yacht racing) to put the products they design through the test. 'Not only are they ambassadors for the brand, they also give valuable product feedback. We often have R&D meetings with the Gill Race Team and our development team, which includes designers and fabric technicians. Everyone is involved which means we come up with the ultimate products.'

To get involved in the sailing clothing manufacturing business, on the design side, it is important to have some kind of design background and qualifications to back it up. But, in other areas such as the business side of a company you may already have sufficient qualities from a previous career, which could include a Business Studies Degree. Either way, it would also pay to have a keen interest in sailing because you'll be able apply yourself more effectively.

Because sailing is such a specialist sport and there are companies out there including Gill that have spent years building up a world class reputation in this relatively niche market, setting up your own company to produce sailing clothing is feasible, but will be a challenge. 'You'll either need a huge capital injection at start up, or be prepared for it to take a very long time to establish the business which was the case with Gill,' commented Nick Gill.

> 'I started in a very small way, doing the development, production and sales myself to begin with. Any profits were invested back in the business to enable the next step to be taken. It took 10 years to become established, and 30 years on we are still learning, developing and improving the business and the markets where Gill is sold.

Starting at the age of 22 I had age on my side, and what I lacked in experience I made up with youthful energy. In the early days we had to manufacture everything ourselves in the UK. This is not the case today but ensuring the quality is up to standard, is just as difficult.'

As with anyone who is deeply involved with this business, and who is passionate about their products and the success of their business, Gill says he spends all his time when he is sailing analysing what he is wearing: 'Sailing is in my and the company's DNA and being involved in the sport is a very important part of keeping ahead of the development process. Even if I am not racing and just sailing for pleasure, my brain is still working overtime on the product. I need

Learning the art of rope splicing is a real benefit if you want to work in a chandlery. Photo – Julio Graham.

to work out how it feels, decide whether there are issues to be aware of, and most importantly, work out if there are any areas where there is room for improvement.'

Business-minded sailors who enjoy meeting new people, and have a gift for offering practical advice could be the right material for working in the chandlery business. There are hundreds of chandlery businesses around the country, many of which are based in marina complexes to service the customers who berth their boats there. You'll find other popular locations for chandleries based in busy coastal sailing areas or near/on the premises of large dinghy sailing clubs. Many of these companies, particularly the larger ones compliment their business premises with an on-line mail order service. Companies like RS Sailing, Pinnell & Bax, and Purple Marine that specialise in producing championship-winning racing dinghies, also run chandlery businesses alongside, which means there are always a lot of job opportunities available. As one-stop shops covering the building and fitting out of dinghies, supplying the sails, rig tuning, service, and repair, having skills in any of these areas, including retail experience to work in the chandlery, will put you in a good position when applying for a job.

Martin Wadhams – Managing Director of RS Sailing, a company which employs 23 members of staff – says what matters more than paper qualifications is a knowledge of the sport and a knowledge that is relevant to the role they are looking at.

> 'Going for a sales role for example, they need to know the market, the customer and understand the products and ideally have experience or knowledge of how to sell.
>
> We tend to employ more junior level staff from university but that is not to say we wouldn't be interested to hear from those from other careers, because we would simply look at the merit of what they could bring to the company in terms of expertise. It is also really important for those applying for a job to demonstrate a passion and commitment to the sport.'

Setting up your own chandlery business is also worth considering, especially if you can find a niche area in which to build your business. But be careful to target the right market because there's little point – unless you intend to run the business mainly through the Internet – setting up a dinghy racing chandlery in the middle of a boat yard full of cruising yachts, and vice-versa.

Andy Ramsey, who went from being a car mechanic, to a sailing instructor to working in a chandlery decided to purchase his own chandlery business in Burnham-on-Crouch. Over the years he spent in the retail business he felt he had built up enough experience to go it alone so in 2009 made the break and took over an existing chandlery business at Rice & Coles

A busy chandlery like Yachting Solutions means working full time on the shop floor. Photo – Sue Pelling.

Boat Yard in Burnham-on-Crouch and renamed it Yachting Solutions. Chatting to Ramsey about making the break, he said:

> 'I got to the point where I needed to decide whether to buy a house or set up a business and I chose option two because the housing market was plummeting. I had an opportunity to take over the existing chandlery in the boatyard and try and improve the business there. What it needed was a manager to take it over and transform it into a good business. It was risky but I could see the potential. The way I looked at it was if you have a chandlery in a boat yard you are always going to cover your costs because generally those who keep their boats there like to support the business particularly because it is so convenient.
>
> Because you rely on custom from the boat yard you have to be totally dedicated to running the business which means you have to open seven days a week. There's no

point closing up on a Friday evening and opening again on Monday morning because weekends are the busiest times.'

Running a company like this single-handedly is challenging but is something Ramsey knows goes with the territory. After two years of business he now earns enough to employ five on a part-time basis. 'Overall I am really pleased I made the move to go it alone. The first year I met my target and the following year was up 72 per cent, which was a real boost. So, yes, if you think you have found a niche and have the right qualities to go it alone, then I would highly recommend it.'

The **hardware** companies that design and build marine equipment such as deck gear and navigation/communications equipment, winches, paints and coatings, and rigging, make up a large part of the industry so anyone with an engineering or design background with an interest in how systems on yachts work, would do well to look into this sector. Those with a **sales** background and who are knowledgeable enough to talk about and sell marine equipment ranging from winches to buoyancy aids could be well placed to work for one of the many distributors. A visit to either London or Southampton Boat Show would be a worthwhile exercise if you are considering going into sales because you'll find most of the major companies that supply marine equipment will be exhibiting, so you'll be able to get an idea of the sort of companies you need to be investigating.

Yacht insurance and finance are good markets to consider if you've spent time working in similar fields. Although knowledge of the market, and experience in the insurance or the finance industry is important, an interest in boating is also important. At Navigators & General the Brighton-based company, which specialises in yacht and motorboat insurance, most of the insurance staff are boating enthusiasts which means because they understand the products they insure and they are able to offer a more efficient service.

Although there are insurance exams providing formal qualifications, these are by no means compulsory because this industry is more about knowledge and experience in both fields, and having good communication skills.

Working for one of the many companies that **transport yachts** such as Peters & May, PSP Marine, or Dockwise can be an interesting career to get involved with either in management, operations, sales or marketing. In a company like Peters & May, which employs 100 staff in eight countries and in some cases, handles over up 8,000 boats a year, there are plenty of job opportunities available. The company says it is often looking for bright, communicative individuals to join their team and there are even opportunities abroad at their overseas offices.

Jobs at Peters & May, for example, range from administration, marketing and logistics to physically loading boats on vessels. One of the most exciting areas, particularly if you are passionate about

The ground staff at Peters & May working hard to load the America's Cup yacht Team New Zealand onto a plane. Photo – Peters & May Global Boat Transport Specialists.

racing yachts, is the on-demand air freight service the company offers for racing yachts. Richard Howartt, Logistics Manager at Peters & May, says to do this job you need to be ready to travel at any given moment. 'For a job like this you need to be a practical person and willing to learn the skill of loading yachts. You also should be flexible enough to be willing to fly off at any time.'

The sailing aspect of **sailing schools, charter and holiday companies** including how to train to become a sailing instructor, setting up your own sailing school or charter company, are covered in earlier sections of the book, but if you have skills from your current or former career, that you feel could benefit the shorebased operations of these companies, then it's worth investigating the opportunities.

Many of these companies, which are based in the UK, employ staff in a variety of roles including accountants, managers, human resources, customer service, legal, administration, business development, finance, eCommerce, and procurement. Although for most of these sorts of positions it is not essential to have yachting industry knowledge, a passion for sailing is usually preferred.

Simon Headley was a keen sailor but spent 18 years working as an insurance broker in the City. However, he got to the stage in his career where he felt he needed to change so he quit his well-paid job, handed back his company car and took a job as Ondeck's Business Development Manager.

'It was a huge decision because I had a wife and two young children to support, but my circumstances allowed me to go ahead. Writing that letter of resignation however, was probably one of the most difficult things I've ever done.

I was at a good stage in my life where I'd paid off the mortgage, bought a bit of property abroad to set myself up for the future, so came to the decision that it was possible to take a 50 per cent salary cut, give back my three-month old company car, and pension scheme, to do something I really wanted to do. I suppose what really made me sit up and think and review my career was the fact I lost two relatively young friends to cancer. For me that was a big wake up call. I remember sitting in my City office thinking how will I cope with another 25 years of this before I retire.'

With over 500 **marinas** around the country servicing the yachting community, you may find a job within this sector ideal if you are the sort of person who is prepared to work hard and have a flair for dealing with the public. Some of the largest marinas around the country such as Premier in Brighton berth up to 1,500 boats, which means the workload, including the administration, is vast. The sort of jobs you are likely to find in the marina industry include management, administration, or marina operations such as dockmasters, who oversee berthing as well as carrying out general marina maintenance.

At marinas like MDL which is one of Europe's largest groups with 21 marinas and boatyards equating to over 7,000 berths, and other large marina complexes like Premier Marinas, and Quay Marinas, which are based in locations throughout England, Wales and Scotland, training and development of staff is regarded as extremely important, with those in managerial positions encouraged to take the Marina Institute's Certificated Marina Manager qualifications. For those working in the marina, there's also a marina operatives qualification.

Matt Simms – Marina Manager at Royal Quays Marina, North Shields – whose previous career was in environmental project management, said it's a great lifestyle and he would highly recommend it but it's not all plain sailing: 'Having a business background is an asset but you really do need to be an enthusiastic boating person to do this job. You still get the same stressful situations within this industry. You still have financial pressures, and targets to meet, and a business to run, but you're working in a great environment and that is worth a lot.'

Yacht maintenance at marinas means there's a huge demand for skilled workers with knowledge of how to service yacht hardwear. Photo – Julio Graham.

Sports injury therapists and **personal trainers** who specialise in sailing are becoming more in demand as racing develops into a high- profile sport. Most sailors involved in Olympic class, America's Cup, or even at other levels of the sport, will at some point in their career, be subject to treatment for racing injuries, which means that anyone with a knowledge of sailing who has, or is in the process of obtaining qualifications should consider the options. Some large regattas such as Cowes Week, or championships at some of the hi-performance dinghy classes where muscle strain and injury are not uncommon, the service of a physiotherapist for example is becoming more popular.

Emma Westmacott – former round the world racing sailor – is now a personal trainer and has worked for all sorts of offshore racing teams including Ellen McArthur's Jules Verne, Challenge Volvo Ocean Race Amer Sport team, plus many Olympic athletes – in Australia and the UK. Talking about becoming a specialist personal trainer Westmacott says although it is not essential,

Setting up a sports therapy clinic at places like Cowes Week where there are up to 8,000 competitors taking part in the racing, can be extremely beneficial. Photo – Sue Pelling.

experience in the sport will help: 'It is way more efficient if you have played the sport that you are advising training for, because you will understand the actions required to be skilful, powerful and strong.'

Westmacott says if you work for a team they often don't have huge budgets, which mean the chances are you'll end up doing all sorts of other work too:

> 'Working with teams at regattas is totally dependant on the level of the team and their requirements – they all vary. Many of them have a limited budget, so if you are there all the time, you will be doing other jobs, such as helping shift kit around, or organising the food. With the America's Cup for example, you are only training

the team for a few hours a day with cool down, stretching, and massage so you get involved with other duties. Basically, if you decide you want to specialise in this area, you will have to accept that you will spend 50 per cent of your time doing something other than training – which may not be what you want to do.'

Interesting business ideas

Becoming a sailmaker, boatbuilder, weather router, or designer are careers that have some sort of structure, which, in most cases involves planning, training, qualifying and getting work. Although I am not suggesting the process is by any means easy, the fact there is a clear job description means there's a focus to achieve what you originally set out to do.

Some of the other businesses in the marine industry are not quite so conventional and have, in many cases, evolved through pioneering ideas sparked by the work people have been involved with in the past, in former careers. By putting their ideas into practice and using their entrepreneurial skills, not only has the marine industry benefited from these interesting new businesses, but also many job opportunities have been created because of them.

Environmental projects

Susie Tomson is an environmental manager and the Director of **Earth to Ocean** – a company that she and her business partner established in 2009 – which provides a practical, solutions-oriented approach to managing the interaction of sport, recreation and the environment. The ethos of the company, which specialises in sailing and the environment in particular, is that recreational enjoyment and sporting pursuits can be achieved within environmental limits.

Using her qualifications, which include an MSc in Water and Environmental Management, a PhD in Integrated Coastal Management, her position as an Associate of the Institute of Environmental Management and Assessment (AIEMA), and her previous career experience, Tomson has successfully combined her love of sailing and respect for the elements, with a new career in the marine industry.

Tomson described her career background:

'I have worked as a coastal zone management consultant, marine park manager in the Caribbean, worked for the Chichester Harbour Conservancy, and I sit in a voluntary capacity as a Harbour Board member on the River Hamble. Before setting up Earth to Ocean I worked for the RYA for seven years and during that time I established with our partners – the BMF – the Green Blue, which is an environment programme to raise awareness, conduct scientific research, and identify environmentally friendly products to make boating in the UK as sustainable as possible.'

But how possible is it for those with no environmental background to pursue a career in this sector? Tomson commented:

> 'There is no standard qualification for environmental management so there are a variety of MSc programmes out there, and probably taking one of those courses like Kate, my business partner did, would stand you in good stead.
>
> Having experience of business management however, is a useful skill to have and often a more commercial background enables you to be able to converse on a level with businesses trying to make ends meet. Where business is concerned it is generally about being resource efficient and ensuring compliance with legal requirements. Equally, having people skills is vital too. Much environmental management is about managing the human interaction – after all if there were no humans interfering we wouldn't need any environmental management.'

Tomson says the range of opportunities in this sector is endless with ideas including scientific research – biological sampling, and surveying. 'There might also be openings in technology development or project managing development of new environmental technologies – the renewable energy sector particularly in the marine field is rapidly expanding.'

Medical Support

Although it might seem obvious that medics who have an interest in sailing would do well to get involved in the marine industry and work as an event doctor or become an advisor, interestingly there is little demand in the UK. According to Dr Spike Briggs and Dr Mark Tomson who run **Medical Support Offshore** (MSOS), for a long time it was accepted that doctors in the UK would give their time and expertise to 'sporting' events free of charge, but Dr Briggs says the situation is changing:

> 'In a move away from amateur 'Corinthian' style of sport, to a universally more professional model (with financially much at stake) together with a more litigious medical environment, doctors are placed in an increasingly difficult position.
>
> Following the example of motorsport and football most noticeably, I took the decision a few years ago, that in exchange for the medical responsibility that I was taking on, I needed reasonable recompense. The result was MSOS, a legal entity that was identifiable and responsible.'

Using their skill as medics and their knowledge of sailing, the two doctors got together, found a niche in the market and now run a successful medical support unit. 'Essentially we have made the path ourselves, following our own ideas, and attempting to give our clients the best service we can, to ensure their racing or adventure sailing continues uninterrupted.'

The company Medical Support Offshore provides comprehensive support for offshore sailors by designing and supplying medical kits for racing teams, expedition boats, and leisure cruisers. They are the medical advisors to the Volvo Ocean Race, the Velux 5 Oceans Race, and the Global Ocean Race as well as many of the UK's top solo sailors such as Dee Caffari, Sam Davies, Miranda Merron, Brian Thompson and Alex Thomson. They also run training courses for crew using the kits. One of the important aspects Doctors Briggs and Tomson provide is the 24-hour cover for crews using the kit. Dr Tomson, speaking about an incident said:

> 'An Open 60 returning from the Caribbean with four young crew onboard got knocked flat in 50 knots of breeze and the two lads down below fell 17 feet from the top bunk, one breaking his arm and the other breaking his knee. The phone went in the early hours of the morning and over the next few days we were able to nurse them home to the Cape Verde islands where they could get hospital care. This included 'walking' them through giving morphine injections, splinting the leg and immobilising the arm, and giving the correct analgesia and antibiotics to prevent infection. There was also a positive psychological benefit of talking to someone who understood the issues that they were facing out at sea.'

Dr Briggs' advice for doctors (Junior or Senior) contemplating getting involved in the sailing industry:

- First and foremost, get experience of sailing at the sharp end, both inshore racing and offshore.
- Don't just go as the medic – be identified as a good sailor first and foremost and use your skill when necessary to gain valuable experience.
- Get experience and qualifications in trauma medicine. Emergency Medicine is ideal.
- A diploma in Sports Medicine is also worth the effort.
- There are quite a few wilderness medicine courses to consider taking such as Medex, Wilderness Medicine Training which offer invaluable training for when practicing medicine far from definitive help.

Internet boat berthing business

With a passion for sailing and with a keen eye on technology, innovative entrepreneurs James Steward and Charles Bacon were able to put their ideas and expertise together to create **The Waypoint** – an internet-based business, which enables the automatic posting of temporary berth vacancies at marinas. Their idea is to give mooring owners, such as marinas, harbourmasters, and boat owners, a platform in which to coordinate the letting and sub-letting of berths.

Charles Bacon, co-founder of The Waypoint, created the concept after experiencing first-hand the problems facing boat owners and marinas when it came to berth vacancies. He believes it could become a crucial aspect of a marina's strategy to maximise revenue in the future.

The revenue from this business however, will ultimately come from marinas who sign up to be part of the scheme which means there is potential to expand the business and take on more employees.

Time Share Sailing

SailTime is an American company that was founded in 2001 and introduced to the UK at its Hamble base in 2004. There are now 15 European bases, which offer what is known as fractional sailing. The idea is for sailing enthusiasts, who don't want the responsibility of owning their own boat, to become SailTime members, which enables them to benefit from a yacht share scheme.

Each SailTime base is independently owned and operated by a local entrepreneur who provides a service. The company is seeking to expand its network even further in Europe, which means if you are passionate about sailing, and have the drive and commitment to manage your own business to the highest possible standards, a company like SailTime could be an option.

Interestingly, John Bostock did exactly that. He was a successful business professional holding key sales, marketing and general management roles in American Express, Diners Club and Thomas Cook, and was European Vice President for the American Express corporate card division, but had an idea that led him into a new career.

As a member of a similar scheme for cars, Bostock said he felt there must be a way to make the scheme work for sailboats and powerboats so started to look into the possibility of setting up something. 'In my research I discovered SailTime had already found out how to do it, so I jumped at the chance to bring the idea to Dorset.' Bostock is now European Managing Director, handling all aspects of SailTime in Europe, UK and Ireland.

Finding a job

During the process of deciding in which area you would like to specialise it is advisable to keep an eye open to see what job opportunities are available. The demand for different types of skills varies depending on the economic state of the market, which means thorough research is vital. There will be times when engineers, and skilled woodworkers for example, are in demand, so it would probably make more sense to go down that route rather than pursuing an area where there are more qualified staff looking for work than there are positions available.

Checking out the job vacancies on company websites is a good start because not only will you instantly see the sort of jobs on offer but you'll also get an idea of the sort of salary you are likely to earn. Most of the larger companies such as Sunsail, OnDeck and Neilson also have career sections, which allows you to scan the job vacancies and see if anything appeals. Having a chat or arranging a meeting with the staff member of a company that deals with recruitment can also be worthwhile.

In the UK, one particularly useful resource that provides an instant indication of what's out there is www.marineresources.co.uk. The site offers a comprehensive marine recruitment service covering all aspects of the sport including the leisure marine sector and gives a good feel for the market.

Chapter 8
Media

Working in yachting media, whether in journalism, public relations (PR), photography, television, or radio, is probably one of the least structured areas of the industry. It is also one of the fastest moving areas of the marine business with technology creating big changes in the media world. Magazine and newspaper staff are now expected to be multi-skilled across a variety of media. Being able to write well for print titles may no longer be enough – editorial staff will find themselves getting involved in creating audio and visual content for websites, and adapting to different styles of writing from news, blogs, features to book writing skills.

For this, media qualifications to learn about the technology are highly recommended, but because sailing is so specialist, the priority in sailing journalism is to have a genuine passion for

A scoop of journalists gather for a media announcement during an America's Cup promotional event at Cowes Week. Photo – Sue Pelling.

the sport. It's not that you need to be a superstar sailor to be able to write knowledgably, it's the fact that you have to be able to talk the 'language.'

As with most specialist sports, knowing your subject will give you a real head start because you'll be able to write without worrying about tripping up on the jargon. It is easy to identify a writer not specialised in the sport when you find the odd word in a feature completely out of context. If you are a sailor and you do have that passion, then it will come through and the readers won't even think twice.

If you are a keen, knowledgeable sailor, sailing journalism can be one of the most fulfilling and exciting areas to be involved in because you are effectively being paid to indulge your passion. And because more than likely you will, by the very nature of the job, be covering high profile events, you'll get the chance to visit some of the most amazing places on the planet, and meet your sailing heroes.

Having spent most of my working life as a yachting journalist covering most of the world's premier events from dinghy racing championships to the America's Cup, I feel privileged to have had the chance to meet and interview many of the world's most respected sailors. Although there are too many examples to mention, one of the most significant that I have been fortunate enough to meet and interview was the great Paul Elvström at his home in Denmark. Elvström, who is now in his eighties, won four successive Olympic Gold medals and will live on to be known as one of the great sailing legends of our time.

Written Journalist

Ideally then, to become a yachting writer you should have a sound knowledge of the sport and industry as well as a good command of the English language. If you are a journalist from another sector, and are keen to learn and become passionate about the sport of sailing, then that is an extremely good start.

Matt Sheahan who is the Racing and Technical Editor at *Yachting World* magazine said that learning the language is a priority.

> 'Being knowledgeable about what you are writing about is the most important thing to consider. You can learn to write, you can learn to present, and learn all kinds of other techniques that won't take as long as learning to be a lifetime fanatical sailor. I think people underestimate the knowledge you need to have to be a sailing journalist. That is why so many people do media studies and come out the other end thinking they like the idea of writing about sailing, but in my opinion, it's never going to work.'

A magazine editor's job is never done. Here David Glenn – *Yachting World* editor – juggles phone interviews with writing editorials. Photo – Sue Pelling.

Although this may be bad news for those with media qualifications and not much passion for sailing, it is good news for those who are not quite so academically minded but are passionate sailors. Sheahan who has been working as a journalist for 20 years now, added:

> 'I wasn't the slightest bit interested in writing at school, but I've ended up being a journalist and that was after I went down the yacht design route. In my opinion there are two things that made it possible; the first is because I was so passionate and had a lot of knowledge of sailing. You don't need to be any good, just extremely keen. The second thing is word processing, without that I don't think I could have done it because I don't have a streamlined enough train of thought to make a typewriter work.'

If becoming a freelance yachting journalist is your aim, getting a job at a publishing house, which produces specialist sailing titles and websites is highly recommended. Not only will you get a thorough insight as to what goes on in the publishing world and learn a lot about the industry, you'll get the heads up on the sort of stories magazines are looking for which could help you in the future as a freelance. Jobs in these sorts of specialist magazines and websites however, are sought after which means when a position is advertised, the response rate is usually high.

As a freelance journalist you'll need to do a lot of background work by offering magazines and newspapers your feature ideas. You'll find the more you know about the publication, and knowing who to contact with your suggestions, the better, but this still doesn't guarantee you'll get an immediate response, or the response you were looking for. When you do get signed up to write a feature however, make sure you get written confirmation from the commissioning editor before you go ahead, explaining the terms agreed including number of words, details of payment, and copy deadline.

Becoming a yachting journalist, particularly in the freelance world, is definitely not a 'get rich quick' business but it does offer a generally good lifestyle. You'll also have plenty of opportunities to get involved in the sport, which means occasionally there'll be a chance to actually go sailing. A lot of these opportunities are created by PR companies keen to gain as much exposure for their clients as possible. If that means inviting a group of journalists on a press trip and giving them a fun and informative time and an opportunity to demonstrate their product or event, in the hope that something positive will be written about it, then that's what usually happens. In most cases these events are extremely worthwhile because not only can you learn a lot about the client, product/event but you'll also get a chance to network with other journalists.

One of the most exciting press trips I've ever experienced was when I worked for *Yachting World*. Andrew Bray the then Editor, offered me his place on a press trip to the Omega-sponsored Bob Sleigh World Championship in St Moritz to compete against the likes of Ellen MacAthur, Russell Coutts (four times winning skipper of the America's Cup), and Mateusz Kusznierewicz (Polish Olympic Finn gold medallist). However, it was on the first bend of the St Moritz CeIerena bob sleigh run, doing 135 mph, upside-down in a flimsy four-man bobsleigh, when it dawned on me the reasons why my boss had 'kindly' given me his place on the press trip. Thankfully I lived to tell the tale and it was a lot of fun, and as far as 'sailing' press trips go, quite unique.

Author

Becoming a full-time author for a living may sound like a dream job if you are a talented writer and knowledgeable about the sport, but in reality there isn't really any serious money to be made out of writing yachting books. Even if you do produce a best seller, it probably won't make much of a difference to your life in financial terms.

If you do decide you have what it takes to write sailing books however, keeping your mainstream job is extremely advisable. Even authors who produce endless streams of books, generally have a back-up career to supplement their income. Tom Cunliffe, who writes authoritative sailing text books including the invaluable Shell Channel Pilot, and The Complete Yachtmaster, supports his book writing career as a feature writer, lecturer, TV presenter, consultant, sailing teacher and expert witness. He says that even if you have a string of different titles in print, you are never going to be able to give up your other work: 'I for example, may be a successful author but that doesn't mean I am a rich author, and writing books is certainly not the passport to riches and idleness. For every person like J.K. Rowling who makes a lot of money out of it, there are thousands that don't.'

The way to view writing books is to use it as a vehicle in which to raise your profile and make the other job you do, more marketable. If you establish your credibility by writing books that are well received it will certainly do you no harm, and you might get a lot more work as a result. Cunliffe endorsing this view concluded: 'Books bring you to the public attention and are important as part of the whole package. If you become a successful author it will make your day job much more successful because it can lead to all sorts of other interesting work.'

Websites

Although most publications have their own websites and are generally staffed by those who work there, some are run independently employing one or two editorial staff and a website technical specialist to ensure they run smoothly. The general perception of websites however, is they can virtually run on their own with minimal staff but in reality the concept of running a website should be no different from a magazine, with an advertising, technical, and editorial staff in place to ensure the content is not only of the highest standard, but constantly updated. Because very often however, there is perhaps only one person running the content section of the website, it is one of the most demanding areas to get involved in, so if you do decide to pursue a website journalism career, and you get a job running a website singlehanded, keep a check on your work/life balance because you may find it takes over your life with free time becoming words of the past.

Radio and TV

As with written journalism, having a sound knowledge of sailing is one of the most important factors when working in radio or TV. Even if you decide to go down the technical route, which doesn't involve presenting, you'll still need to know one end of a boat from the other. And depending on the type of job you are thinking about, it generally pays to have some form of media training to give you a firm understanding of how programmes are produced and edited.

In the marine filming industry the jobs available include runners – who carry out odd jobs and look after the production team, producers, presenters, cameramen, and directors. Andrew Preece, who switched his yachting journalism career to work in the film industry is now the

A cameraman needs a good sense of balance when filming during racing. Photo – Sue Pelling.

Executive Director of Sunset and Vine, the company that supplies most of the sailing coverage to the BBC including all the Ellen MacArthur footage when she broke the world speed record, Olympics, Vendée Globe, America's Cup, and the Volvo Ocean Race. Being frank about the type of candidates he would consider to work on his team, Preece said:

> 'We liken ourselves to racing crews, who look for a great team with energy who are willing to go that extra mile. Some of the most important jobs in this business are the run-around type jobs. For this we need doers with a good level of initiative and practical skills. We need those who can drive RIBs and build sets. But more than anything, we look for those who know about sailing. An understanding of the sport to know what's going on is imperative in all aspects, from run-around to production.'

One of the most skilled jobs for any sailing film team is a camera operator because not only do they need to be extremely good at their job but also they should be in total harmony with sailing. Preece continued: 'It is important they have the ability to get on a boat without getting tangled up in the mainsheet, know exactly where to stand, and be aware of what's going to happen next. I have spent a lot of time filming aboard yachts and it's not easy by any means particularly on fast, hi-tech racing yachts. As well as being able to cope with being onboard a boat they also need an eye for filming. The eye is harder to teach than the technical side of things. Having the ability to see a shot and understanding what a good frame looks like is important. Some people are better than others for no particular reason.'

Becoming a TV presenter is an immensely skilled job and the openings available for full time positions are extremely rare. *Yachting World*'s Technical Editor Matt Sheahan also works as a presenter for TV during the America's Cup but admits the presenting business is like a 'lucky dip' and opportunities are rare. 'There are two types of sailing presenters; the headline/familiar face presenters who the broader public know and who try to bring the sport to the masses, they are the ones who draw the public in. Then there are the sport specific presenters who have a good command of the technical side of sailing. Yes, there are opportunities out there for sports specific or technical presenters but they are so few and far between when you look at the small amount of coverage sailing gets on TV.'

Public Relations (PR)

If you have the ability to write well and persuasively, and have knowledge of the industry, you might consider working in the PR arena. The industry has many companies specialising in the marine sector including those covering major events, products or personalities. Some of these companies are independently run and have a small yet manageable client base. These companies occasionally employ extra staff to help out when running big events for example, so it is worth doing research to find out what opportunities are on the market.

Some of the larger agencies such as Into the Blue – a sports marketing, PR and events company primarily focused in the areas of sailing, extreme sports and environmental sponsorships – employ over 20 staff to cover their accounts. This company, which is based in Cowes on the Isle of Wight, was established in 2005 by Jo Grindley whose previous work included being a freelance consultant to Volvo Car UK, along with the commercial management of Ben Ainslie and Shirley Robertson's Olympic sailing campaigns. Talking about setting up the business and the risk involved, Grindley said: 'I had money to put into the business, so I had no need for a bank loan. Consequently it didn't really feel like a risk – just a natural progression. I also knew I had the knowledge within the business sector, skills and creativity to deliver to our clients, so that helped too.'

Setting up your own sailing PR company is an option but it is a relatively small yet highly competitive market, so to start with it would be more sensible to seek employment at an established

PR agency that specialises in sailing. This way you get more of an idea of what's involved and work out if you think you could make a living from running your own agency.

To work in sailing PR, knowledge of sailing and the industry would certainly help. Grindley says that learning about the industry as well getting experience in jobs that will help take you where you want to go is vital.

> 'I served my apprenticeship by working as a freelance journalist, sailing TV news producer, managing a photographer's library, and working as a consultant on the Volvo sailing sponsorship programme. In that time I learnt a lot about the business including dealing with feedback, even negative, and using it to progress. Being honest about what you can deliver is also something people will respect you for.
>
> Because PR is all about the clients, you will need to have good organisational skills, no ego, and the ability to switch your mind from creative to analytical and forward plan. I, for instance, am never worried about today, tomorrow or next week – but I am constantly worried about two years ahead!'

Photographer

Making a successful living from yachting photography is possible but can be a huge challenge. If you market yourself correctly and become good at what you do it can be one of the most exciting job options on offer. Depending on which area you specialise in, you could find yourself heading off to some of the most interesting places in the world, taking photos from helicopters and mixing with some of the greatest sailing legends on the planet.

One of the biggest hurdles in the early stages of a photography career is making a name for yourself, and like many areas of the marine industry, it's all about building up a good reputation as someone who is not only good at their job but who is also flexible and willing to work hard and deliver.

Having an interest and a talent for photography is, of course, a priority but knowing about sailing and having an eye for a good publishable action shot is also something to consider.

Richard Langdon who runs his own independent photography company – Ocean Images – has been into shooting sailing since 1988 but admits he is hopeless at what he considers is the most important aspect of the business – marketing. He believes that he would have reached the top level a lot sooner had he embraced marketing more effectively: 'One of the most important things and actually something I consider myself useless at is my own PR. I seriously think that is why it took me so long to make it. Although I am now established, through my skills as a photographer, I realise now how important it is to market yourself correctly regardless of how good you are.'

Avoiding camera shake in rough conditions is one of the obstacles facing yachting photographers. Photo – Miles Kendall.

Like many leading yachting photographers have found, the last five years has seen significant changes in the industry which have altered the way photographers work. In the past, a whole host of yachting photographers would turn up at an event and take thousands of images in the hope their prize shot would be snapped up by a magazine or newspaper to at least cover the cost of expenses and hopefully a bit more. Now it's all about who can bag the biggest sponsored jobs.

Langdon says that although you'd be a fool not to take a sponsor-backed job that will pay good money, he is concerned it has affected the variety of shots that are now available. 'Working for a sponsor where the photos you take are copyright-free, means magazines, websites and newspapers are reluctant to use anyone else's photos, so it's hardly worth any other photographers turning up. I personally think it is a shame because it has tinted the variety of shots taken at events. Before you used to have six or so photographers going out to Antigua Classics or Cowes Week for example all shooting from different angles, now you generally only get the one event-employed photographer.'

According to Matt Dickens, founding Director of onEdition Photography which specialises in marine/ocean racing photography covering a variety of events such as the Artemis Transat, Barcelona World Race, JPMorgan Asset Management Round the Island Race, VELUX 5 Oceans, World Yacht Racing Forum, Monaco, there is always room in the market for new faces. 'It is important to remember however, that from the outset you need to establish who your clients are and who is paying you, don't just bob about hoping to earn a living because that is never going to work. My advice is to get a job working for other photographers, even just as an assistant, because this is an excellent opportunity to get a good grounding before you specialise in one area.'

Chapter 9
Yacht delivery

There is a constant need for professional delivery skippers, which means getting a job in this sector is a good option if you have the right qualifications. It can also be a lucrative career if you plan your seasons well, and get yourself known as a reliable, trustworthy operator.

Private deliveries for owners who want to get their yacht from one destination to another, maybe for a regatta, to a charter destination, or who want the new yacht they've just purchased sailed home, are some of the most popular reasons professionals are called in.

Yacht deliveries are also required by yacht builders or brokers who need to transport vessels to and from boat shows around the globe, or need to deliver yachts to new owners or charter companies.

A delivery skipper enjoys perfect conditions as he rounds Cape St Vincent, off the Portuguese coast. Photo – Professional Yacht Deliveries Ltd.

Becoming a yacht delivery skipper is one of the most rewarding jobs because there's a great sense of achievement once you've successfully completed a delivery. You'll also get the chance to sail some exceptionally smart yachts of all sizes to some of the most interesting and exotic locations in the world and get paid for it. So, if you are someone who enjoys variety and travelling, and who doesn't mind spending weeks away from home, yacht delivery is a great option to consider.

Most professional yacht deliverers work on a freelance basis, either independently or sign up to a yacht delivery agent who basically gets the jobs for them. Most work on daily or lump sum rates with the skipper paid the most. At PYD (Professional Yacht Deliveries) for example, a skipper can expect to be paid between £90–£150 per day. In most cases, the skipper is the only person among the crew who gets paid, but because yacht deliveries are often to far flung destinations from the UK to places like the Caribbean or Med, there is a good opening for those who are in the process of training for exams and who need to build up their mileage log. This is also a good way of seeing how yacht delivery works, first hand, and to give you the opportunity to see if you are cut out for that sort of career.

The best way to go about volunteering for such a trip is to make contact with a yacht delivery company and see what's available. Phil Coatesworth – Director of PYD – says they always have plenty of volunteers keen to clock up miles on delivery trips. 'As well as our large pool of professional skippers we have several thousand crew volunteers on the file to choose from.'

When you take on a position as skipper of a delivery yacht, the responsibility is immense because not only are you in full charge of someone else's yacht, but you are also responsible for the crew you take with you. You are also likely to face adverse conditions out on the high seas which means you could have to be on watch 24 hours a day, so you'll need to be competent enough to handle not only the sailing, but the long, challenging hours too.

Qualifications required

It goes without saying that if you are going to be taking full charge of someone else's yacht, you need certain levels of qualifications to allow you to do this. Essentially, you need to have your RYA Yachtmaster Offshore certificate to qualify as a skipper and, of course the relevant experience. Phil Coatesworth says that although it is absolutely necessary to have the right qualifications, you also need the right personality:

> 'As skipper you must have Yachtmaster Offshore as a minimum and sufficient experience to convince us on an extended skipper's trial (where you are on board as mate to regular skipper) that you have the necessary skills and personal qualities. 15,000 nm is about the minimum, but most have much more. Mates must also be Yachtmaster qualified whilst deckhands are expected to be Day Skipper or higher although the ability to stand a solo watch at night is the benchmark.

Although experience is important, what we look for is people who are prepared to work hard coupled with high personal standards.'

An interesting training option offered at PYD is a Sailing Apprenticeship Scheme which is a six-month programme to ensure recently qualified Offshore Yachtmasters have the required level of experience and competence before they go it alone as a yacht delivery skipper. It is basically an opportunity to gain valuable experience as a Mate to a variety of experienced PYD skippers under a structured and thoroughly assessed programme over a minimum of 10,000 nautical miles of sailing worldwide.

Trevor Vincett who runs TV Yachts for World Deliveries says that other than having all the right qualifications – i.e. no less than an RYA Yachtmaster Offshore – experience is what takes priority when he recruits skippers.

'I tend to take on skippers who've had a lot of experience, often those who are a bit older who know the coasts and ports well. You have to be 100 per cent sure a skipper is capable because you can't afford to make mistakes when in charge of other people's yachts. One of the best ideas for those who want to gain experience is to sail as mate on an apprenticeship basis. For this I would say you need at least your Competent Crew certificate. Going as an apprentice will not only build up mileage and experience in all aspects but you will also get used to making decisions, and get an idea of what's in store when you take on a role as skipper.'

Bryan Walker retired on medical grounds following an injury in the fire service in 1996 but decided to turn his passion for sailing into a new career. He obtained his RYA/MCA/DOT Yachtmaster Instructor Ocean certificate and has been delivering yachts for PYD for over 10 years. He says that a yacht delivery career offers a great lifestyle but you do need to have certain qualities to get the most out of it. 'Delivering yachts can be challenging and rewarding at the same time but does provide great job satisfaction. You get to meet lots of people from all walks of life so you need to be able to socialise with them on and off the water. Being a good communicator and able to pass on information and build confidence with the crew is also very important.'

Walker is clear about the need to acquire qualifications: 'It is really important to get your Yachtmaster qualifications, but gaining some teaching qualifications will open a lot more doors and enhance your sailing skills.'

Yacht safety checks – what can go wrong

Taking charge of a yacht that you know nothing about including its history is potentially risky so you need to be aware of the issues to look out for before you set sail. For a start you need to find

One of the most important jobs of a delivery skipper is to run through the safety check list before setting sail. Photo – Professional Yacht Deliveries Ltd.

out if the yacht has all the up-to-date paperwork that provides evidence it meets the required safety standards.

If you work independently as a freelance yacht delivery skipper, you'll need to handle all these sorts of issues yourself, and have the ability to turn down a job if you are not satisfied the yacht reaches the required standards. However, if you work for a yacht delivery agent, all the admin and documentation will be dealt with by the company, leaving you, the skipper to make the final checks and observations before you set sail.

At PYD – one of the UK's leading yacht delivery companies – Coatesworth says before he agrees to anything, he has to have confidence in the yacht's condition. 'A boat has to be "fit" and seaworthy taking into account the passage involved. We need to know there's an in date life raft and flares are on board. An EPIRB is required for offshore trips, and a satellite 'phone (which we may provide) for ocean crossings. Beyond that there is a contractual warranty on the part of the owner to ensure safety and general fitness, and we very occasionally walk away from a delivery if we are not able to achieve the necessary standards.'

Although most modern, glassfibre yachts are built to standard and therefore generally create little cause for concern, yacht delivery companies are often wary of classic boats because until the crew actually turn up for the job, they don't really know what state they will find the yacht in.

Trevor Vincett says you often only have limited information before you travel to the yacht. If you get there and the boat is a wreck and you don't go ahead with the job, you need to be able to cover your costs. 'Whenever we are travelling abroad we always get a big deposit up front and travel expenses because from our point of view if you get there and the boat is a total heap of rubbish, not fit for purpose, we wouldn't touch it. Thankfully, in the 30 years I've been involved in yacht delivery I am pleased to say I've only had to refuse one job, when the boat was a complete wreck.'

Vincett said there was an occasion when they had a problem with a classic boat they were supposed to be bringing back to the UK from the Med. This yacht had been out of the water, sitting in the sun for a couple of years and all the wooden planking had shrunk. 'It was terrible because by the time the crew got out to sea, the boat was leaking like a sieve. The crew had to return to port and hose the boat down for a day to make the planking take up water and expand. It was fine after that. But it just goes to show, you have to be wary of old, wood boats, and you need to find out as much as you can about them before you set off.'

Bryan Walker added: 'Preparation is one of the most time consuming aspects of the job because you have to be sure the yacht is totally seaworthy. We normally spend at least 24 hours checking the condition of the yacht and all the equipment on board to make sure it all works properly and is in date of any servicing due. This is one area where proper preparation really needs to be thorough.'

The other potential problem when delivering yachts is the weather. When a delivery job is booked in advance, the weather is an unknown factor, which means careful monitoring of the weather is essential before you set off for the job. You may still find you turn up at a job and are forced to delay the departure time and end up sitting in port for days on end waiting for the conditions to moderate. The weather can also take its toll – with too much or too little wind – once you are out at sea, which can often cause delays, particularly in places like the Atlantic. Walker continued: 'I suppose that is one of the negative points of the job. You generally know roughly how long the job will take but it all depends on the weather. Delivery jobs regularly take 3-4 weeks, but one of the longest for me was six months.'

Private versus yacht delivery agency

Working as an independent yacht delivery skipper gives you the freedom to be your own boss, decide which jobs to take on, and it gives you the chance to earn a full salary without the agency taking its cut.

Although there is the chance of earning more money by working for yourself, it's worth considering the advantages of working for a well-run yacht delivery company which include the security of knowing you will get paid for the job, and having central management back up for travel, crew allocation, spares and weather advice. Coatesworth says a yacht delivery company will do a lot of the background work:

> 'A well managed delivery involves taking a great deal of care in preparation and protection. We rely on exhaustive pre- and post-delivery check lists as part of the process. However, even quite a short delivery can involve more miles than many

> boats otherwise do in a year, and as a consequence poor maintenance, often over the life of the boat, can show itself. We actually have relatively few problems, but skippers need to be very resourceful in coping, often without good local support available. The most preventable and regularly occurring problems of all seem to revolve around fuel contamination.'

By choosing to go with an agency you'll also get the benefit of their marketing skills and finding suitable jobs to befit your experience. At PYD there is a pool of 35 qualified skippers on the books, which means when a job comes up, the company allocates the most suitable candidate to take on a job.

Trevor Vincett runs a slightly smaller set up with a nucleus of about six professional skippers and says the admin is a big part of a delivery job and something *he* handles: 'I get the jobs, price the jobs, do all the administration then leave it up to my skippers to carry out a professional service and take a commission from them. It works well this way and everyone knows where they stand.'

How much could you earn?

As with all jobs in the marine industry the amount you earn from yacht delivery depends on the individual job, what's involved, and whether expenses are included in the overall sum. Vincett continued:

> 'It very much depends on the location and the type of yacht because in the Med for example it is very expensive to provision for a trip. And the other big expense is travelling. Going to airports, and travelling on trains and buses in Europe is expensive, so that has to all be built into the overall cost. A transatlantic delivery – from the UK to the Caribbean – is about £6,000. On this sort of trip you are at sea a lot of the time and not spending money berthing the boat or in and out of airports. Being at sea is pretty cheap. I budget for about £6 per person per day for provisions. A skipper therefore might earn £5,000 for an Atlantic job, which might take him anything from four to six weeks.'

Index

Index compiled by Annette Musker